MY BODY IS GOOD

EMBRACING BODY POSITIVITY AND GIVING UP DIET CULTURE FOR LENT

ANNE CUMINGS

UPPER ROOM BOOKS®
NASHVILLE

At the time of publication, all websites referenced in this book were valid. However, due to the fluid nature of the Internet, some addresses may have changed or the content may no longer be relevant.

Cover design: Emily Weigel
Cover imagery: Zaytseva Larisa / Shutterstock
Interior design and typesetting: PerfecType, Nashville, TN

Print ISBN 978-0-8358-2010-3
Epub ISBN 978-0-8358-2011-0

For Hazel,
who I hope will grow up never needing this book.

CONTENTS

Before We Begin 9

Introduction: Word & Flesh 11

Paczki Day. 21

Ash Wednesday 24

The Bread Body 27

Look at the Birds 29

Strawberry Donuts Forever 31

Sunday: Anti-Diet Is Not Anti-Health. 33

WEEK ONE

The Life Thief. 37

The Real American Idol 40

Diet Culture Fails the Test. 42

Who's Talking? 44

Losing Weight Won't Heal the Hurt 46

Move with Joy 49

Sunday: Finding Body-Positive Community 51

WEEK TWO

Powers and Principalities 55

Your Body Is a Temple. 58

CONTENTS

Approach Health with Wisdom 60

Make Peace with Your Body 63

Spiritual Health Is Health Too. 65

You Are Not Alone. 67

Sunday: Creating Body-Positive Icons 69

WEEK THREE

Eating for the Glory of God. 75

Body Diversity Is Beautiful 77

Bread of Life 79

God Had a Body 82

You Don't Need to Be Perfect 84

Inherited Diet Culture. 87

Sunday: Spiritual Body Mapping. 89

WEEK FOUR

What Will We Pass Down? 95

Living in a Resurrection Body 97

All Food Is Morally Neutral. 99

Salvation Came Through a Woman's Body 101

There Is a Body for Every Season 103

All Bodies Are Good Bodies 105

Sunday: Watch Your Words. 107

WEEK FIVE

You Can Trust Your Body 113

Feed Yourself 115

CONTENTS

Forgive Yourself 117

You Are Not Too Much 119

It's OK to Have a Bad Body Day 121

Body Freedom 123

Sunday: The First Supper 125

HOLY WEEK

Eat Like a Kid Again 133

Spiritual Hunger 136

Body Privilege 138

Maundy Thursday: God Loves You, Feet and All. 140

Good Friday: Body Love in the Shadows 143

Holy Saturday: Body Justice. 146

Easter Sunday: Freedom Has Always Been Here 148

APPENDIX

Resource List 153

Notes 155

Contents

HOLY WEEK

ADVENT

BEFORE WE BEGIN

This book is intended to be a healing space for you to examine your relationship with your body. As part of this conversation, issues of food, exercise, body image, mental health, and discrimination are addressed. If you are struggling in any of these areas, I highly recommend seeking out a mental health and/or medical professional to help you on your journey. A good place to start is the Find a Therapist function on the *Psychology Today* website. This search engine lets you sort by location, race, gender, therapeutic model, insurance coverage, and areas of expertise. Visit https://www.psychologytoday.com/us /therapists for more information.

INTRODUCTION

Word & Flesh

The altar had been stripped of all things shiny and polished, and rough gray muslin and burlap had taken their place. Instead of the bright lights of Sunday morning, homemade paper lanterns were strung up to warm the darkness of a late winter Chicago night. In the flickering shadows of candlelight, I made my way to the front of the small stained-glass-adorned sanctuary. I could smell the oil mixed with the ashes gathered from burning last year's palm branches as my pastor pressed the gritty mixture into my forehead in the shape of a cross. "Remember that you are dust, and to dust you shall return." I am dust. I am made of earth. In that moment my earthiness, my fleshiness, my body itself became something holy.

The religious tradition in which I was raised is not big on bodies. I was taught that flesh was something to be conquered and transcended. Giving into the desires of my body was a slippery, sinful slide into debauchery. Whether it was what I ate or drank, how I dressed, how I moved, or—God forbid—who I touched and how I touched them, my body was trouble. According to the church of my youth, the Christian life is about the spirit, and my physical body is just the shell that carries me around until I die and escape it.

In contrast, the culture around me screamed that my body—or should I say having the "perfect" body—was exactly what made me acceptable and lovable. Advertisements, magazines, TV shows, movies, music—all of them bombarded me with images of the perfect body. A perfect body ought to be thin but not too thin. Sexy but not too sexy. And I was constantly being sold makeup, hair products, clothing, diet products, and diet plans—all with the goal of attaining that perfection.

So when I found myself at the altar on that Ash Wednesday and felt the warm thumb of my pastor on my forehead, something shifted. I became aware that there is no way for me to be a Christian without my body. It was my body that moved through that sanctuary, my body that sang the longing, penitential hymns, and my body that watched as candles flickered on the altar table. It was my body that smelled the oily ashes spread on my forehead as a tangible, sensory reminder of my humanity.

Yet all those messages telling me my body was bad were—and sometimes still are—circling through my being. It has taken many years of the Holy Spirit whispering something new into my soul for me to consider that maybe, just maybe, my body is good. After all, God created us in her image and, reflecting on her creation, called us very good.

Lent is a season focused on the body, a time of reflecting on the ways God shows up in human flesh, especially in the person of Jesus. But even in a religious tradition that is based on God taking on human flesh, so many of us use Lent as a time to deny our bodies. We give up sweets or meat with a secret hope of losing weight. We take on fitness challenges, claiming the guise of spiritual discipline while in our hearts hoping to work our bodies into submission. This book means to challenge that mentality. It says yes to the body and to the spirit, claiming that there is no way to separate them to begin with. We are word *and* flesh.

Let's spend this Lenten season settling into our bodies instead of punishing them. Let's sink our hands into the cool spring soil and remember that we come from the earth. Let's connect with the ways our bodies both hold and reveal the Spirit. Let's worship our Savior who was both divine and human, who was both word and flesh.

What This Book *Is*

This book is intended to create a healing space for you to reconnect with your body and with God. I hope that the daily meditations will offer you a moment to practice a body-positive mindset and allow you to linger with the idea that your body is good. Each day you will find a scripture passage to ponder, a reflection, and a prayer. I encourage you to journal after each day's reading. I find that journaling allows me to process new ideas and capture questions, feelings, and thoughts that arise. You will also find embodied spiritual practices throughout the book. These exercises are meant to help you go deeper in understanding the impact our culture's obsession with thinness has had on your spirit, to allow God to heal the wounds left in its tracks, and to form a new relationship with your body and your spiritual life.

What Is Body Positivity?

The term *body positivity* may be new to you. At its root, body positivity is a social movement that makes this claim: All bodies are good bodies. It says no to our mainstream culture that values thin, White, heterosexual, cisgender, able-bodied bodies over and above all others. The body positivity we discuss in this book is not a shallow affirmation of our appearance or a platitude that can be captured in an Instagram post. Body positivity, in this book, is an act of radical self-love. Sonya Renee Taylor, author of *The Body Is Not an Apology*, defines radical self-love as a life-giving foundation for relating to our bodies and to our society. She writes, "Radical self-love is deeper, wider, and more expansive than anything we would call self-confidence or self-esteem. It is juicier than self-acceptance. Including the word *radical* offers us a self-love that is the root or origin of our relationship to ourselves."[1]

The word *radical* means "going to the root or origin." In Christianity, our origin goes back to the moment God created human bodies and called them good, yet somehow Christianity veered far from those roots. Body-positivity activists have been working for body diversity in all areas of media and culture since the 1960s.[2] However, Christian circles have been slow to adopt this type of thinking. Christian culture has promoted thinness, weight loss, and subjugation of the body as moral imperatives, using concepts like purity, self-control, sinful gluttony, and others to teach us that we must deny ourselves and our desires. In my experience growing up in evangelical Christianity, I was taught that my body was something to be conquered and subdued. My body and its needs or desires could not be trusted. In order to grow closer to God, putting my body in its place was necessary. Spirit before flesh. My body was certainly not something to be enjoyed, celebrated, or even just left to its own devices. Whenever I slipped up and fell into the flesh, shame was heaped on in mounds. Professor and writer R. Marie Griffith describes American Christian culture's emphasis on bodily subjugation in her book *Born Again Bodies: Flesh and Spirit in American Christianity.* She writes, "Disregard what goes into your body, many suggest, and you will not only gain weight, look ugly, and feel awful but you will also doom yourself to a lifetime and likely an eternity of divine disfavor."[3] Thinness was next to godliness.

In spite of the many attempts of misguided Christians to demonize the body, Christianity is a body-positive faith. We worship a Savior who had a body. And we worship in and through our bodies. Barbara Brown Taylor writes, "What is saving my life now is the conviction that there is no spiritual treasure to be found apart from the bodily experiences of human life on earth."[4] That is why a Christian, by nature, *should* be body positive. The body must be understood as good because it is all we have to experience the Divine. It is all we have to feel with, to relate with, to heal with. We are stardust infused with the very breath of God. God's creative action permeates our every molecule with the spark of the Divine. Theologians and philosophers like to talk about body, mind, and spirit as though they are clearly defined and separate entities. That is nice as a thought experiment, but in our everyday lives we don't experience our minds or spirits outside of our bodies. We talk about emotions as "gut feelings." When we experience stress, we get headaches and digestive problems, and our muscles tighten. Sometimes a spiritual experience is accompanied by shivers and tingles. John Wesley, founder of Methodism, famously talked about his conversion experience as feeling his heart "strangely warmed." As much as we might like to transcend our bodies completely, our bodies are where God has chosen to meet us. At the first Creation, God breathed life into matter; in Christ, God took on a body to meet us in our humanity. Christianity is inherently body positive.

Body Positivity Versus Body Neutrality

As the body-positivity movement has progressed, some have made the claim that body *neutrality* is a more optimal goal. Body neutrality shifts the focus from what our bodies look like to what they do. It also makes important space for the reality that feeling "positive" about our bodies is not always possible in the moment. Proponents of body neutrality seek to take our minds off our bodies all together. They also offer feeling neutral about our bodies—that is, not good or bad—as a more attainable goal. It can be difficult to go from loathing your body to finding joy and beauty in it. Neutrality can feel like an easier perspective to ask of ourselves. In general, I don't see neutrality as superseding positivity but as a part of a broader ethos of body positivity. Body neutrality directs us away from focusing entirely on what we look like, which is great. But I believe bodies are beautiful—all of them. And I believe God sees our bodies this way too. We don't have to see our bodies this way or feel beautiful in every given moment for this to be true. In any case, rejecting the beauty of the body seems like a rather bland solution.

I also believe considering the body as good, rather than neutral, is important from both a theological perspective and an emotional healing perspective. We do not need to be walking around in every moment obsessed with the beauty and wonder of our bodies. That's just silly. We will not always like the way we look or love what our body does or does not do. But we can trust our bodies to breathe and move and feel in ways that God built into us for our good. We need our bodies to heal, to worship, to make art. And, yes, also to eat and to do sexy things and to dance like no one's watching. The outcome of body positivity when aligned with spiritual practice is embodied spirituality, healing, wholeness, and joy.

What Is Diet Culture?

Those of us in the United States live in a world that is obsessed with thinness—especially when it comes to women's bodies. I recently pulled some data for the community surrounding the church I serve, and one statistic jumped off the page at me. In a survey on what life concerns are most important to people, losing weight was second on the list. The only item listed higher was financial concerns. Losing weight was more important to survey responders than their stress level, having a satisfying job, experiencing romance or intimacy, having time for family and friends, or finding direction in life. Moreover, losing weight was far higher on the list of concerns than personal health problems or a health crisis/illness.[5] Diet-culture rhetoric is frequently disguised as a "concern for health." But this study shows that people are far more concerned with being skinny than being healthy. This is diet culture. Prioritizing losing weight over a happy marriage or a fulfilling job is diet culture. Prioritizing losing weight over actual health is definitely diet culture—and also unhealthy.

Registered dietitian, podcast host, and author Christy Harrison defines diet culture as "a system of beliefs that equates thinness, muscularity, and particular body shapes with health and moral virtue; promotes weight loss and body reshaping as a means of attaining higher status; demonizes certain foods and food groups while elevating others; and oppresses people who don't match its supposed picture of 'health.'"[6] Diet culture includes all the implicit and explicit messages around us that tell us thinness should be our priority when it comes to our bodies. It is the advertisements and magazines that only show us photoshopped images of beauty as they try to sell us the latest weight-loss fad. It is the almost $80 billion weight-loss industry that thrives by making us feel insecure while simultaneously selling us products that will not work. It's realizing the weight-loss products aren't working but blaming ourselves instead of the industry. Diet culture is elementary-school-aged girls worrying about being too fat and starting diets before they are even through puberty. It is the widespread discrimination that bigger people experience, from name-calling and cruelty to having to navigate spaces that are inaccessible. It is the erroneous belief that one must be a certain size to be healthy. It is putting thinness above mental and spiritual health.

Diet culture is all this and more. I hope this book will offer you space to become aware of and to dismantle the messages diet culture is sending you. It's time to allow your body to release the shame it feels and to reconnect your body to your mind and spirit. I hope this season will be a time for you to say yes to a life of body liberation.

What This Book Is *Not*

This is *not* a book about weight loss. It doesn't include workout tips or healthy recipes. I understand why you may be looking for those things, but you won't find them in this book. In fact, you are going to find a great deal of information about why a focus on weight loss is not healthy for your mind, your spirit, or your body.

In order to heal from diet culture, I believe it is important to create a space that is protected from it. As you are working through this book, try to steer clear of messages that tell you something is wrong with your body. This includes diet plans and fitness fads and books, Instagram accounts, TV shows, movies, and office talk that prioritize weight loss. Be selective about what you expose your heart to during this time. Additionally, I encourage you to actively seek out body-positive messages. There are many books, social media influencers, and podcasts that address body positivity and will inspire you in this journey. I compiled a list of some of my favorites in the back of this book to get you started.

Why Write Just for Women?

You may be thinking, *Men need body positivity too!* And to that I say, yes, of course they do. However, women have borne the brunt of negative messaging about their bodies since Eve ate whatever fruit was in the Garden. Much of what drives body negativity is rooted in the ways women's bodies have been made into objects of desire. Reflect on how a woman's body used to be considered the actual property of her father, male relatives, or her husband. In ancient marriage arrangements, women were bargaining chips used to forge alliances and build familial wealth. A woman's value was based on what kind of family allegiance she could secure to insure her family's legacy and how many babies she could provide to keep the legacy alive.

Additionally, because of the history of slavery and racism in this country, Black and Brown women also deal with the devaluation of their bodies because of the color of their skin. Dr. Sabrina Strings draws a distinct connection between fat phobia and the history of slavery and racism in the United States in her book *Fearing the Black Body: The Racial Origins of Fat Phobia*. She writes, "The fear of the imagined 'fat black woman' was created by racial and religious ideologies that have been used to both degrade black women *and* discipline white women."[7] Springs posits that as slavery continued in the United States, fatness became associated with Black femininity and was used as a way to devalue the lives of Black women while maintaining the false superiority of White women. As racism and white supremacy continue to plague our nation, Black women must contend both with overt and covert racism and with a fat phobia that is rooted in our society's fear of Blackness.

While most of us now choose our own marriages and are no longer bought or sold based on the value of our physical body or our family's wealth and power, the history of this objectification lives on. Women's bodies, more than men's bodies, are deemed "hotter" or sexier or more desirable when they match up with cultural beauty norms. Our ability to attract the dominant male gaze is equated with our worth. Men, on the other hand, are stereotypically valued by their financial means, their athleticism, and their accumulation of power and prestige, which is another issue for another book. Men can be paunchy, and we see them as having a cute dad bod. They can get gray and wrinkly, and we see them as distinguished silver foxes. Even so, this issue is not cut and dried, especially as we continue to work for gender equality and affirm the experiences of queer and gender-nonconforming people.

I am encouraged by the presence of many non-binary and plus-sized people in the media and in my own life who are shattering these archaic, dualistic ideas about what types of bodies are attractive and valued. But there is still a gaping canyon of inequality when it comes to how we perceive and value men's bodies, women's bodies, and non-binary bodies. All the more reason women need a healing space to discuss body positivity through the lens of a loving Creator God. We need a space where we can seek to undo what the world has taught us about our bodies and begin to understand them as good—not because they are sexual or social currency but because they are created by God.

Paczki Day

Some call it Shrove Tuesday. Some call it Mardi Gras. And others call it Pancake Tuesday, but the good Polish people of the Midwest call it *Paczki* Day. *Paczki* (pronounced Poonch-key; *paczek* in the singular) are decadent fried doughnuts filled with jelly or custard, and they are what I eat on the day before Ash Wednesday. I've read that in Poland the quintessential *paczki* are filled with rose hip marmalade, glazed with icing, and sprinkled with candied orange peel. In Poland, *paczki* are actually eaten on Fat Thursday, the Thursday before Ash Wednesday, which kicks off a whole week of indulgence before Lent begins. I'm not sure how the weeklong feasting got pared down to one glorious day in the United States, but we still have our *Paczki* Day, and I choose to savor it.

The traditions of indulgence surrounding the days before Lent consist of consuming all the sugary, rich, boozy goodness we can before we enter into a time of penitence and fasting. In the day or days leading up to Lent, we prepare for the scarcity that is to come. For those of us who have internalized diet culture our whole lives, these celebrations can trigger feelings associated with all those ill-fated "last suppers" we scarfed down before embarking on the latest diet trend, cleanse, or fitness routine. This Lenten pattern of indulgence and then restriction is all too similar to cycles of yo-yo dieting and bingeing and purging.

Beyond those issues, scarcity and deprivation are at the heart of dieting, so preparing for a liturgical season that calls for the exact same things can bring on all sorts of emotions and impulses. You may be secretly hopeful that this season will finally be the one that you resist chocolate and easily slip into your Easter frock. Or you may be dreading another failed attempt at restricting yourself for forty days. Even those who have engaged in healing work around their relationship with their bodies may be reminded of old wounds and lies that feel as though they will threaten their progress. Whatever your physical, emotional, and spiritual responses are to your preparation for Lent, give space to them and know that you are not alone. If eating a *paczek* (or any other food) on this day feels celebratory or as a way to honor your body, do it. If you find yourself worrying, *But this is the last doughnut that I can eat until Easter!*, then I offer you a different way to engage with your body and with the Spirit on *Paczki* Day.

Shrove Tuesday is perhaps the most liturgically official name for this day. The word *shrove* comes from the word *shrive*, which means "to absolve" or "to free from guilt." What if we used this Tuesday to recognize all the guilt we have been carrying about and in our bodies? All those times we berated ourselves for eating "sinful" foods, those times we looked in the mirror and heaped shame and disgust on ourselves, those times we compared ourselves to others and said terrible, nasty things to ourselves—let's bring all of that into the open and let it be absolved. Let the Holy Spirit wash over every inch of our skin and gently caress all the guilt and shame away. We don't deserve that guilt anyway. There is nothing inherently bad about eating delicious food. There is nothing sinful about having a bigger body. If you have a hard time believing that now, let me hold that belief for you over the next forty days.

Though tradition may tell us that Lent is a time of fasting, God did not invent Christian liturgical traditions, nor does God require that we adhere to them. So I suggest something other than fasting this year. Spend some time today setting an intention for this spiritual season. What needs healing? Where do you need repentance? Consider how you've been unkind or even abusive to your body that you need to turn away from. How have you felt anger toward your body or jealousy toward the bodies of others, and how can those feelings be expressed or shared with a trusted friend and healed? How has diet culture robbed you of a vibrant life and joy? Let your heart wander through all the feelings and emotions that arise. Listen for the Spirit whispering what she desperately wants for you and your body. When you land on something that feels right, jot it down in a journal or on a sticky note that you can return to over the next forty days. Let's spend the season of Lent listening to our bodies and learning to love them as God does.

I'm going to go find some *paczki*!

Ash Wednesday

"By the sweat of your face
 you shall eat bread
until you return to the ground,
 for out of it you were taken;
you are dust,
 and to dust you shall return."

—Genesis 3:19

A sh Wednesday is one of my favorite days in the liturgical calendar. Does that make me seem like a sad person? I mean, who likes thinking about their own sin and mortality? I consider myself someone who always sees the glass as half full, someone always looking on the bright side. Because of my optimistic nature, I tend to be more surprised than I ought to be when I encounter people being the sinful messes that all humans are. But Ash Wednesday pulls me back down to earth. It grounds me in my earthiness—both the fact that we are all created from dust and that we will return to it. It allows me to sit with the presence of sin and suffering. So much more so than Easter Sunday, Ash Wednesday feels human to me. It feels imminent and embodied. It is about our physical bodies and all their limitations. But it is also about our bodies as the only vehicle we have for experiencing life and the Divine.

As a pastor, I have the sacred privilege of imposing the ashes on others. As I stand at the front of the sanctuary, people of all shapes, sizes, genders, ages, races, ethnicities, sexualities, and abilities present themselves, and one by one I mark them as holy. It is an intimate moment. When I press my thumb into the silky, paper-thin skin of an eighty-year-old woman and declare, "From dust you came and to dust you will return," I consider all the wisdom and experience held in her body. Declaring the same over a small child, wiggling under the motherly hands pressing into her shoulders, serves as a reminder of all the precious opportunities life holds. What could this little girl learn from the eighty-year-old woman? What inspiration does the young girl hold for the matriarch? What might this middle-aged pastor learn from both? Pressing ashes on those beautiful foreheads is like pushing a holy reset button that reminds me of our common humanity.

I don't know where you stand on Ash Wednesday, whether you love it or hate it or are indifferent to it. Regardless, it is the starting point for this journey. Ash Wednesday is a moment to reflect on your relationships to your body. Spend some time considering where your relationship with your body stands today. What lessons were you taught about your body growing up? These lessons may have been implicit or explicit. You may recall things you learned from your family, friends, or relatives; you may remember things that you absorbed along the way simply by being a person in the world.

Here are some questions to help guide your reflection:

- What kind of food rules did your family have growing up?
- How did you hear your parents or other important people in your life talk about their bodies?
- How did your parents or other important people in your life talk about bodies in general? How did they talk about your body?
- What was your relationship with food as a kid? with exercise?
- When, if ever, did you start to question the goodness of your body?
- How did you make a connection in your early years between your faith and how you relate to your body?

- What do you remember learning from your faith community about bodies in general or your body in particular?

God of new beginnings, help me to
acknowledge, perhaps for the first time,
the beliefs about my body that I have
held for so long. Guide me in sorting
which beliefs are helpful and which are
harmful. Lead me back to you and
to this body that you called good. Amen.

The Bread Body

I will give them one heart, and put a new spirit within them; I will remove the heart of stone from their flesh and give them a heart of flesh.

—Ezekiel 11:19

My flour-covered hands sank into the dough as my body bobbed and swayed with each push. I watched as the dough took shape, absorbing the flour I had scattered on the countertop. And in the middle of my kneading, I noticed the dough taking the shape of a heart totally by accident. Not a perfectly shaped one that we would see on a child's Valentine but a messy lump of ventricles and atria, veins and arteries. This squishy, weighty blob would soon be baked to a golden goodness.

My bread almost never turns out perfectly. I have visions of a crisp crust decorated with beautifully scored designs. But most times the score doesn't work and the bottom bursts open or I bake it a little too long or there's not enough steam in the oven to get that perfect chewiness. But no matter how it looks on the outside, my bread almost always tastes amazing. And each moment I spend with my hands in bread dough reminds me that my heart is in each loaf.

Like my hands in the dough, I feel God leaning into me, creating me, molding me into something perfectly imperfect, infused with love and light. So many times, I have fretted about the shape or size or imperfections of my body. But God delights in me. No matter how many times I have scoffed at my reflection or berated myself for my lack of self-control, I remind myself that I am God's creation and God's heart is in me.

So maybe I can extend myself the same joyful grace I extend to my bread. Maybe I can see myself as perfectly imperfect. Let's rejoice in the God who created us in love.

> Creator God, help me remember that you have placed your heart in me. Continue to knead my heart into something warm that beats with love. Amen.

Look at the Birds

"Therefore I tell you, do not worry about your life, what you will eat or what you will drink, or about your body, what you will wear. Is not life more than food and the body more than clothing? Look at the birds of the air: they neither sow nor reap nor gather into barns, and yet your heavenly Father feeds them. Are you not of more value than they?"

—Matthew 6:25-26

We spend so much of our time worrying about our bodies. One morning, I found myself sitting at my kitchen table squeezed into pants that were a size too small, berating myself that they didn't fit as they once did. I cycled through the same thoughts—what would I eat for breakfast, what would I eat for lunch, what would I do when I needed an afternoon snack, what would I do when my friend invited me to dinner, and on and on. Suddenly I heard birdsong float through the window. Just outside on my suet feeder was a gorgeous chartreuse pine warbler. My thoughts shifted, and I penned the following words:

Worrying about being too fat or not pretty enough is really quite boring. When I think of all the time I spent fretting about such things and not noticing the yellow-bellied warbler in the tree above my head, I feel silly.

When I think of all the creative, funny, smart souls I missed, my mind preoccupied with the calories/grams/carbs on the table between us, I feel sad.

When I think about the books I didn't read, the music I didn't discover, the art I didn't seek out because my emotional energy was used up on body loathing, I feel regret.

When I think about the lost moments in the sun, not noticing the exquisite way the sand felt and the rush of salty water because I was hiding under a flattering cover-up, I feel longing.

And when I think of all the ads, the bombardment of images, the generational passing down of toxic body beliefs, the hurtful comments, and the objectifying culture that trades real, interesting, funny, smart, sexy women for fantasy images, then I feel angry.

Today I noticed the warbler.

God of the warblers, you take such loving care of your creation. Help me remember that I am part of that creation too. I don't need to worry about my body or what I will wear because I am loved and cared for just as I am. Continue to send your birds to remind me that beauty and song come in all types of bodies. Amen.

Strawberry Donuts Forever

"You have pain now, but I will see you again, and your hearts will rejoice, and no one will take your joy from you. On that day you will ask nothing of me. Very truly, I tell you, if you ask anything of the Father in my name, he will give it to you. Until now you have not asked for anything in my name. Ask and you will receive, so that your joy may be complete."

—John 16:22-24

One day a donut robbed me of my joy. It was a beautiful spring day, and my family and I had driven through the hilly North Georgia countryside to a little farm with some chickens and goats and field after field of strawberries. The kids ran through each row of strawberries in their overalls, plucking berries and shoving them in their mouths until the sticky, red juice ran down their chins. The air swirled with the scent of homemade strawberry donuts, and pretty soon the kids started begging for one. And who was I to say no?

I purchased our donuts, and we plopped down at a wooden picnic table in the shade. As I stared at the warm, pink, speckled donut, anxiety filled my chest. My kids ate their donuts quickly and went on to examine the animals at the farm, but I ate mine slowly, guilt—or was it shame—bubbling under the surface. I felt myself teetering at the edge of the slippery slope that beckoned me to obsess over what I was eating. I heard a voice in my head berating me. I tried to respond with, *It's just a donut*, but the voice didn't listen.

Is it ever just *a donut?* she retorted. *After this donut, then what? Aren't you just going to keep eating? Aren't you going to get fat?*

And there it was. Even though I talk the talk and mostly walk the walk, deep down I know I'm afraid of getting fat. As if being fat is the worst possible thing in the world—as if being fat is a bad thing in the first place. This fear lurks deep inside me, and I'm not always consciously aware of it. But it's the voice of internalized fat phobia, and she is a liar. In that moment, fat phobia was actively trying to steal my joy. The joy of being present with my family on a beautiful day. The joy of enjoying a delicious treat filled with strawberry goodness. The joy of satisfaction, contentment, playfulness, and pleasure. The joy of being fully human in my body. That voice wanted to steal it and replace it with guilt, shame, grief, and deep sadness. But Christ offers a different voice—one that says "Silence!" to fat phobia and the lies of diet culture.

Recognizing our internalized fat phobia involves deep grief and fear—grief over how we have treated ourselves and others as we've participated in diet culture and the fear of becoming or staying fat. Once we have acknowledged that grief and fear, their realities and the way they affect us every day, we can make room for the joy that is available to us. Acknowledging that grief and fear and choosing joy doesn't mean we will never struggle or experience self-loathing. But Jesus promises that no one gets to take our joy—not ourselves, not someone else, and not even a warm strawberry donut.

God of strawberry donuts, you promise a joy that no one can take away. When the voices of self-loathing are loud within me, stirring up feelings of guilt, shame, and anxiety, remind me of that promise. Amen.

Sunday

Anti-Diet Is Not Anti-Health

One of the most frequent responses I get when I talk about being anti-diet or anti-intentional weight loss is the accusation that I am anti-health. The idea that health is equivalent with thinness is so ingrained in us that to suggest a focus outside of weight loss is perceived as a rejection of health in general. This is absolutely untrue. So what does it look like to be healthy? Some might say eating fruits and vegetables; others say exercising. But there is so much more to taking care of your health than just food and exercise! Spend some time thinking about all the ways you can take care of your health that don't involve trying to change your size or shape. Then pick something and do it! Here's a list to get you started.

Ways to Support Your Health That Don't Involve Weight Loss

- Listen to music
- Go to therapy
- Wash your hands
- Spend time with a friend
- Go to bed early
- Hug someone you love
- Drink a glass of water
- Take a stretch break
- Say no to something you don't have time or energy for

- Say yes to something you want or need
- Laugh
- Sit in silence
- Read something for pleasure
- Learn a new skill
- Play a game
- Make a budget
- Schedule a preventative healthcare appointment
- Go to the dentist
- Dance in your living room
- Pray
- Buy clothes that fit
- Spend time in nature
- Have sex
- Make art
- Sip a cup of tea
- Make a special meal
- Read scripture
- Call someone you love

WEEK

one

The Life Thief

"All who came before me are thieves and bandits, but the sheep did not listen to them. I am the gate. Whoever enters by me will be saved, and will come in and go out and find pasture. The thief comes only to steal and kill and destroy. I came that they may have life and have it abundantly."

—John 10:8-10

Registered dietician, podcaster, and author Christy Harrison talks about diet culture as "the Life Thief."[1] This phrase perfectly describes the way our society's obsession with thinness steals our lives from us, moment by moment. When we could be enjoying our lives or be present to the concerns that truly matter to us, we instead are fretting about what our bodies look like or how we can restrict or control our behaviors in order to change them. Diet culture can even change the way we remember our experiences.

I once worked with a woman in my counseling practice who came in to see me after she went on a beach vacation with her friends. She was refreshed and glowing with joy from being out in the sun and surf and spending time with people she loved. In particular, I noted the way she talked about how much joy she experienced in her body. She gushed about basking in the sun, sticking her toes in the sand, and playing in the ocean.

The following week she came to see me again, and in the time between our sessions she saw pictures of herself at the beach that were posted on social media by one of her friends. Her entire energy had changed. She talked about how disgusting she looked and how she felt like a fool for being out on the beach in a bathing suit. I was startled by how differently she now remembered her vacation. Her memories of a relaxing, fun, and joy-filled experience were replaced by feelings of shame and self-loathing. It was the same vacation, but seeing the pictures through the lens of fat phobia and diet culture changed her actual memory of it.

Diet culture told this woman that bodies like hers don't deserve to feel the sun on their skin or the salty spray of the ocean. It told her that her body was shameful. Like a thief, diet culture stole the experiences she had of physical pleasure and emotional connection with friends and the earth. The Life Thief of diet culture "comes only to steal and kill and destroy" (John 10:10).

Today's scripture passage from John describes Jesus as a sheep gate. It says that those who follow Jesus and listen to his teachings will find safety and nourishment in the green pasture. Listening to Jesus means ignoring the voice of the diet-culture Life Thief. While the voice of diet culture tells us our bodies are wrong or bad, the voice of Jesus hearkens back to Genesis and says our bodies were created in God's image and are not just good but *very good*. When the voice of fat phobia tells us that we don't deserve to enjoy delicious food or frolic in a bathing suit, the voice of Jesus says we belong in the nourishing green pasture—or on the sandy beach—no matter our shape or size. Jesus came so that we "may have life and have it abundantly." Let's listen to the voice of Jesus and truly live fully by saying no to the Life Thief.

God, you are the gateway to an abundant and joyful life. Forgive us for listening to the Life Thief of diet culture that only seeks to steal from and destroy us. Remind us that our bodies are created by you and that you desire for us to live a life free from the lies of body shame. Amen.

The Real
American Idol

"You shall not make for yourself an idol, whether in the form of anything that is in heaven above or that is on the earth beneath or that is in the water under the earth."
—Exodus 20:4

f you have spent any time reading through the Hebrew scriptures, you likely have noticed a pattern with the ancient Israelites. These folks could not make it more than a few weeks without finding or creating an idol to worship instead of God. Take, for example, the freshly liberated Israelites in the wilderness after they escaped bondage in Egypt. After all they had experienced, they make it to Mount Sinai, and Moses goes up the mountain to meet with God. Moses stays on the mountain with God for forty days. Mind you, God had just miraculously saved Moses and the Israelites from enslavement by parting the Red Sea, by leading them around the desert with pillars of cloud and fire, and by dropping bread from the sky and making water come out of a rock. And still, after not even six weeks, the Israelites wonder if God is dead and ask Aaron to make them a new one to worship from melted gold. Why did they do this?

As humans, we are prone to worship something. Even people who say they aren't religious or don't believe in God will find a way to center their lives on someone or something. And when that someone or something isn't God, that's what we call an idol. Writer Michelle M. Lelwica suggests that for modern Western women, the idol of choice is thinness.[2] If we are worshiping the idol of thinness, we will create rules and rituals and communities around that idol. And we will believe that idol can offer us salvation.

It's easy for us to point fingers at the ancient Israelites and say, "Of course a golden cow statue wasn't God!" But it is not hard for us to believe that being thin will be our salvation, that being skinny will be the answer to all our problems. So many of us have believed that if we could just stick to the rules of dieting and force our body to shrink to some magic number on a scale, then we would be happier, healthier, more successful, more loved, and so on. We may not realize consciously that this is what we have believed or currently believe, but our actions point to it. I say this not to shame us for making thinness an idol. We are surrounded by diet culture and pervasive messaging that tells us thinness is not *next to* but *is* godliness. And the ancient Israelites were in the same boat. Everyone around them was worshiping multiple gods and creating physical idols to worship. It is hard to choose truth and go against the status quo. It is difficult to say no to the dominant culture around us and to stay true to the God who really does offer salvation and liberation.

And that is good news: While thinness does not offer salvation, God does. When we can step away from our belief that thinness is the answer to all our problems, we are able to see what God already offers us no matter the shape or size of our bodies. God calls us beloved and worthy of good things—not because of our size but because we are children of God.

Lord, forgive us for making thinness an idol. Give us the courage to go against the grain and center our lives on you, rather than on shrinking our bodies. Help us to see the freedom you have for us when we set aside the idol of thinness. Amen.

Diet Culture
Fails the Test

Beloved, do not believe every spirit, but test the spirits to see whether they are from God, for many false prophets have gone out into the world. . . . Little children, you are from God and have conquered them, for the one who is in you is greater than the one who is in the world.

—1 John 4:1, 4

Don't believe everything you read, they say. But it's hard not to when it seems like every magazine and newspaper article, every headline, and every advertisement says that losing weight is the best way to achieve health. The weight-loss industry in the United States is worth 2.7 billion dollars. Even our doctors, the people we trust most when it comes to health, may urge us to lose weight or ignore our real health concerns, telling us that they would be solved if we weighed less. Some may even purport that losing weight is easy and merely a matter of eating less. But that's simply not the case.

Since 1959, research consistently has shown that at least 95 percent of weight-loss attempts fail, with all the lost weight (or more) being regained within two to five years.[3] Gaining weight is not a bad thing in and of itself, but if the purpose of a diet is to help us lose weight then it at least should be trusted to not do the opposite!

Today's scripture passage from First John talks about discerning spiritual teachers and what they teach about Christ. In the early church, some false teachers were trying to teach a hyper-spiritualized path to God that was completely disembodied. They believed that the goal of Christian life was to transcend our bodies. But the way of Christ is only walked in flesh and blood. New Testament scholar Craig R. Koester puts it this way: "The incarnate Word cannot be reduced to spiritual abstraction. Divine love is not simply an idea. It takes tangible form in the life Jesus lived and the death that he died."[4] God meets us here, in the material, bodily world. In verse 3, the writer calls these teachers the "antichrist." In other words, this way that denies the body is a substitute for Christ, not the real thing. Diet culture asks us to deny our bodies. To deny our bodies' hunger, their natural shape and size, and their needs for rest, pleasure, and emotional care. Following Christ means following truth, and the truth about diet culture is that it is robbing us of the abundant life God wants for us. The truth is diet culture is a false prophet that is selling us a bill of goods.

In the coming days and weeks, I encourage you to "test the spirits" of weight loss. Has trying to lose weight or change your body's shape and size brought you a sense of new life, joy, peace, and satisfaction? Or has a focus on weight and size bred anxiety, shame, self-loathing, or disappointment?

Holy Sophia, God of Wisdom, open my eyes so that I can clearly see the ways diet culture has harmed me. Help me to walk a path of truth that is fully embodied. Help me to say no to the enticing lies of diet culture and to stand firm in the power that lies within me. Amen.

Who's Talking?

Whatever is true, whatever is honorable, whatever is just, whatever is pure, whatever is pleasing, whatever is commendable, if there is any excellence and if there is anything worthy of praise, think about these things.
—Philippians 4:8

This morning I saw a photo of myself that sent me into a spiral of self-loathing. It was a candid shot from an angle I apparently don't see often in the mirror or when I'm staring at myself during a Zoom meeting. Immediately I began criticizing myself. I started comparing myself to my friends and to strangers on the internet whose bodies are smaller than mine. I know that focusing on weight loss harms me emotionally, psychologically, and physically, but being triggered by the photo caused me to question myself. Even though I knew better, I started berating myself for not eating the "right" things and working out every day.

Then I realized I was hungry, and I went into the kitchen. As I stood in front of the cupboard contemplating what I could eat that would be "healthy," a deep sadness filled my gut. My mind had run away with itself. I had spent the last hour or so being so unkind to myself. I had been fixated on all the things I hated about my body and on how I didn't measure up to others. Even though I have immersed myself in the research on the inefficacy and harm of dieting, these negative thoughts hijacked my mind and had me desperate for any way to change my body.

How easily our minds get stuck on whatever is untrue, whatever is mean, whatever is negative, whatever is self-harming, whatever is shameful, and whatever is disrespectful. It seems especially easy for this to happen when we address ourselves in this way. Paul's words to the church in Philippi remind us that we have a choice when it comes to what we focus our minds on.[5] We can come across that photo taken from a less-than-flattering angle and focus on whatever it holds that is pleasing or excellent. In the photo I saw this morning, I was hiking with my four-year-old, and I was leaning on a thick, sturdy tree. There was a sun-kissed lake in the background, and my eyes were glistening with laughter. There was so much beauty around me. I was playfully engaged with my son and the nature around us. But all I saw when I looked at the photo the first time was the way my chin doubled up and the way my stomach looked from the side.

Sometimes, try as we might, we may not be in a headspace to find anything worthy of praise in a bad photo. When that happens, we can choose to put it away and hunt for whatever is pure and pleasing and commendable. Search for something inspiring to read. Choose to follow persons on social media who represent all the diversity found in creation. Walk through the woods and pay attention to the leaves, the mushrooms, and the intricate spiderwebs. Above all, fix your mind on what is true—that you are a beloved child of God, just as you are.

God of all consciousness, forgive me for letting my thoughts rule over me instead of you. Help me to recognize when my negative thinking is harming me. Give me the strength to choose a different focus for my thoughts. Help me to see the things that you see, all that is true and pleasing and excellent. Amen.

Losing Weight Won't Heal the Hurt

When the righteous cry for help, the LORD hears
and rescues them from all their troubles.
The LORD is near to the brokenhearted,
and saves the crushed in spirit.
Many are the afflictions of the righteous,
but the LORD rescues them from them all.

—Psalm 34:17-19

n a world that claims thinness as the highest ideal, so many of us feel we don't measure up. We spend an inordinate amount of time and energy plotting ways to shrink our bodies because we think being thin will make us happy and fix everything that is wrong in our lives. We tell ourselves that when we are thin, we will find love. When we are thin, we will finally like ourselves. When we are thin, we'll enjoy vacations. When we are thin, we won't feel ashamed. On and on goes the list of wounds that thinness will miraculously heal. Buried underneath our hopes of all the problems that being thin will solve are deeper hurts. There is the loneliness and the longing to feel valued; the sadness and the loss that come from being robbed of experiences of beauty and joy in our bodies; the fear that we are not adequate or lovable just as we are.

Perhaps one of the cruelest tricks of diet culture is that these hurts and fears are not assuaged by losing weight. Yes, the world rewards us when we have temporary success with losing weight. We are bombarded with compliments that can feel as addictive as any controlled substance. But the hurts that lie underneath are still there. We still carry with us the painful rejections, the old traumas, and the fears that linger in our deepest, darkest parts. Moreover, at least 95 percent of all people who lose weight will gain it back. Our hyper-focus on weight loss may distract us for a while, but our bodies normally respond to the restriction and rigidity of dieting by gaining back the weight. This is one of the ways diet culture harms us. It convinces us that weight loss is the answer and shames us for not being able to achieve it long-term.

You may feel hopeless. Weight loss may seem like the only answer to the troubles you carry, and giving up on the false promises of weight loss may seem like giving up hope. But there is a better and more hopeful way. Weight loss won't give you love and joy, but love and joy are available to you right now in the body you have. Go on vacation in the body you have right now. Look for love and partnership *now* because you are lovable no matter your size or shape. Talk back to the voices in your head and in the culture around you that say differently. And take your shame and grief to God.

When you cry out for help, the Lord hears. When you are hurting, God will rescue you. When you are brokenhearted and when your spirit feels crushed, the Lord is near. Focusing on weight loss as a solution to your hurts is like chasing a carrot that is always out of reach and then finding out one day that the carrot isn't even what you are hungry for. What you are hungry for is spiritual, emotional, and, yes, physical nourishment. Remember the source of true healing and wholeness is God. When you stop chasing the carrot of weight loss, you can rest in the arms of a loving God and let the real healing process begin.

Healing God, give me the courage to see
the real source of my pain. Help me to
understand that changing my body will not
heal my hurt. Help me to trust in you as the
source of all healing and wholeness. Thank
you for loving me just as I am. Amen.

Move with Joy

*The prophet Miriam, Aaron's sister, took a tambourine in
her hand, and all the women went out after her with tambourines and with dancing.*

—Exodus 15:20

This passage from Exodus occurs just after the Israelites have
escaped bondage in Egypt. God has just parted the Red Sea,
and the Israelites escaped the Egyptian army by the skin of
their teeth. Standing on the sandy beach, bent over, hands on
knees, and hair sprayed wet from the walls of salty water they just passed
through, they take a moment to catch their breath. It takes a minute for
their brains to catch up with what just happened. When the miracle of
their escape starts to settle in, smiles form on their faces and their shoulders lift. They are free!

What is the first thing the women do? They *dance*. They can't keep
still. They move their bodies with joy and celebration. Miriam grabs her
tambourine and leads her sisters in a massive dance party that comes
straight from their hearts. Their dance is a response to being set free. They
dance because God's act of liberation inspires their bodies to move and
skip and prance and jump.

Miriam's dance is a beautiful model for what movement and exercise
can be. I know that exercise won't always feel like an ecstatic riverside
dance of liberation complete with tambourines. Sometimes we move not
because we are emotionally jazzed up about it but because we know it

will make our bodies and spirits feel stronger and more joyful in the end. However, exercise that is laden with the weight of diet culture is a ball and chain. Diet culture convinces us that we need to exercise to compensate for our greedy appetites. When our mind is led by diet culture, exercise can feel compulsive. We stress about when we will make time for working out, and we feel guilty when we skip the gym. Going on vacation means fretting about whether the hotel has a gym or how we are going to get a run in while navigating a new place. But when we let go of diet culture and truly free ourselves from the mentality that sees exercise as a means to a skinny end, we can dance with joy. And not only dance but skip and hike and bike and frolic and splash and dive and paddle and wrestle and bend and flow.

God of freedom, thank you for the liberation that comes in knowing my body is good and loved just the way it is. Forgive me for using exercise as a joyless form of punishment. Help me to find joy in moving and exploring your creation. Amen.

Sunday

Finding Body-Positive Community

When I began my body-positivity journey, I felt as though I was surrounded by people on diets. Once my ears were attuned to diet culture, I heard it everywhere. Wherever two or more women were gathered, diet talk was present in their midst. Something that helped me immensely was finding my like-minded people who were also on a journey of body positivity. At first, books and the internet saved me. I started reading more and more from those who were writing about size inclusivity, intuitive eating, and conquering diet culture. I found social media accounts to follow and started blocking or unfollowing people who spewed body negativity and diet talk. As I started talking about body positivity with friends and family, I began to find some kindred spirits with whom I could engage. I also started my own Facebook group, and it has grown to a couple hundred women who share their struggles, support one another, and post plenty of funny memes.

Finding people who understand body positivity and who will support your decision not to focus on weight loss can be difficult. When you begin sharing your journey toward body positivity, some people won't support you because they have been immersed in what they have heard from doctors, the media, and public health campaigns about "obesity" and all its evils. Some of those people are fat phobic and judgmental. Some may have good, if misguided, intentions. Some may hold a measure of both. Building a circle of body-loving folks around you will require some intentionality.

I recommend starting with the people closest to you. If you are in a relationship, talk to your partner about how they can support you in this journey. Let them know some of what you are learning and ask them to keep diet-culture talk out of your conversations. You can do the same with your closest friends. If you find yourself feeling alone, seeking out online community can be helpful. There are social media groups and accounts to follow that will connect you with women all around the world who are living out a spirit of body liberation. You can even start your own like I did! You can also find therapists, medical professionals, dietitians, and fitness coaches who are body positive.

I have hope that one day there will be a sea change and body positivity will take hold throughout our culture. However, in the meantime, you won't be able to completely shield yourself from diet culture. Diet and weight talk is still a mainstay in many circles women find themselves in. You will hear it in the office, at the gym, at church, at family gatherings, and so on. When this happens, you may choose to respectfully offer your new perspective. Or perhaps you can set a boundary and let the people around you know that you won't take part in conversations about weight. Or you can remove yourself from the conversation entirely. Do what feels right for you.

However you choose to manage those situations, you may come away from them feeling triggered, sensitive, or vulnerable. This is normal, and you are not alone in your feelings. In those moments, I encourage you to turn to your spiritual practices. Breathe deeply, go for a meditative walk, take a healing bath. I recommend choosing something that involves your body. Whatever you do, be intentional about countering the voice of diet culture with the voice of the Divine who has called you beloved.

WEEK
two

Powers and Principalities

We are not contending against flesh and blood, but against the principalities, against the powers, against the world rulers of this present darkness, against the spiritual hosts of wickedness in the heavenly places.

—Ephesians 6:12, RSV

ometimes the voices of fat phobia and diet culture inside us feel loud and powerful. The lies they tell us often feel like truth. We stand in front of the mirror looking at our bodies and feel like the nasty, mean things that we tell ourselves are objective facts. After all, the magazines, the TV shows, and the actual doctors can't all be wrong, can they? Yes, they can. But even when our head has done the research and knows the truth, our heart gets hijacked by the lies. Our heart wants to belong, to fit in, to force our body to match up with what the world tells us is beautiful. This powerful heart-jacking experience can sneak up on us. It doesn't matter if yesterday we were lounging in the sun, rocking a bikini, and loving every one of our curves. The next day something can trigger us, and we can only view ourselves through a lens of self-loathing.

When this happens, I am reminded of what Paul called the "powers and principalities." Throughout his writings Paul talks of these powers as both human power structures on earth and as spiritual forces beyond our material world. These powers and principalities also exist throughout diet culture. Diet culture contains a web of economic, cultural, political, and even theological ideologies that feed us the lie that our bodies (and by extension our whole selves) are not good enough unless they are thin. Struggling against all those forces means paddling upstream. It feels like a true battle. But there is also a spiritual battle within us. It is a battle between God's voice that tells us we are created good and are beloved just as we are and the voice of the enemy that tells us we will never measure up, that we are shameful.

The good news is scripture also tells us that no weapon formed against us shall prosper. God is on our side in this fight, and God's power is mightier than the nasty voices without and within. God's power can defeat social media, discriminatory healthcare systems, the weight-loss industry, and any other principality. So when our heart and mind get sabotaged by fat phobic thoughts and feelings, we can tap into our spiritual power.

I encourage you to find spiritual practices that will build your strength and ground you in the truth of your sacred worth. Those practices can be anything from simply making yourself a cup of tea, to spending time in silent prayer, to turning on some music and dancing in your living room. You might try to write about what's bubbling up inside you or to talk to a trusted friend, family member, or medical professional. Ask a friend to pray for and with you. Take a hot shower and focus on how good your body feels in the water. While the water falls down your back, imagine the Holy Spirit washing away the muck and mire of the battlefield so that you can see clearly again and keep fighting.

God of power and might, sometimes I need your strength to help me battle the voices of fat phobia and diet culture that live within me. When I have difficulty looking in the mirror, remind me of how you see me. Remind me of the truth of my worth. Help me to continue rejecting the powers of this world that want to keep me defeated. Amen.

Your Body Is
a Temple

Do you not know that your body is a temple of the Holy Spirit within you, which you have from God, and that you are not your own? For you were bought with a price; therefore glorify God in your body.

—1 Corinthians 6:19-20

When I was in seminary, a few fellow students and I drove to the Atlanta suburbs to visit a Hindu temple. I had seen pictures of gorgeous temples in faraway places, but my exposure to temples in the United States was limited. I was completely unprepared for what I would encounter that day. As we drove through ornate iron gates, a bright white palace of towers and domes topped with fluttering flags came into view. Every inch of the massive building was covered with intricate detail, and all of it was reflected in a shimmering pool that stretched in front the building. I did not imagine that the inside could possibly match the outside's beauty, but I was wrong. We entered the temple after taking off our shoes and softly stepped into what I imagine being inside a sapphire and looking out might feel like. Blue light reflected everywhere as we quietly walked through a maze of exquisitely carved columns. Vignettes carved into the side of the space created homes for the various deities worshiped in the temple. It was stunning.

Now, whenever I think of today's verse from First Corinthians, I think about what it means for my body to be *that* kind of temple. What does it mean to be something that inspires reverence and awe? How is my body the beautiful, sacred home of the God I worship? How do I relate to my body in a way that makes me want to take off my shoes and recognize the holiness of the ground on which I stand?

I have always been drawn to soaring cathedrals and old churches with big wooden beams and bright stained glass windows. There is something holy in the attention to material beauty as an expression of worship. Tending to our own bodies with this kind of exquisite attention can be an act of worship as well. Rituals of self-care can become sacred. Soaking in a lavender-scented bath, softly and slowly rubbing lotion on our skin, sipping a cup of aromatic herbal tea, walking quietly through the woods, or gently stretching our aching muscles can all become moments in which we meet the Spirit.

Sometimes we struggle to recognize the beauty in our bodies. And I don't think it's realistic or necessary to expect to feel beautiful every moment. But I do believe every one of our bodies is beautiful to God. Your body is a temple. So take off your shoes, pad around in sock feet, and notice what the light looks like from inside your body looking out. You are stunning.

Holy Spirit, help me to see my body as a temple. Some days I don't recognize the sacredness and beauty of my body. But you see it. Help me to see my body as you do and to treat my body as a holy place of worship. Amen.

Approach Health
with Wisdom

*Who is wise and knowledgable among you? Show by your
good life that your works are done with gentleness born of
wisdom.*

—James 3:13

One morning, I woke up with intense anxiety. That happens to me sometimes. Often when it does, I'll grab my phone and try to distract myself from feelings of impending doom. But on that particular morning, I decided to ask myself what my soul needed. My soul's response was surprisingly clear: clay. I wanted clay. I wanted something I could lean my whole body into; something that would give way and allow me to mold it but wouldn't break under my pressure. I needed something that could take a punch, that I could squeeze as hard as I wanted. I drove myself to the craft store and bought some clay and spent the morning molding and smooshing and squeezing. It was just the thing. Strangely, on that morning, what I needed to take care of my health was clay.

Health is not a one-size-fits-all proposition. What is required for health is not only different from person to person but also different from day to day and even from moment to moment. When I'm sick, health looks like resting to allow my body to fight off infection. After a long day hunched over a computer, health looks like stretching the muscles that have been cramped and crouched. When I'm anxious, health looks like doing crossword puzzles and making art and getting into nature. Health can also look like eating foods I love and moving my body. Both bring me joy—and both eating and moving are necessary parts of life.

But when "eating healthy" and "working out" were strictly about weight loss, they were drudgery and guilt inducing. I felt like I had to eat the same way and exercise at the same intensity day after day. Days off were called "cheat days," as if I were doing something wrong when I took a day to rest or eat something diet culture deemed "unhealthy." However, when I began to view health from a wholistic perspective that includes mental health, spiritual health, pleasure, and satisfaction, it became dynamic, engaging, and enjoyable.

Approaching health in this way requires wisdom. We must consider what is needed from moment to moment, rather than applying the same rule or practice to every situation. Scripture shows us the need for this type of wisdom. For example, Proverbs 26:4 says, "Do not answer fools according to their folly, or you will be a fool yourself." But the very next verse says, "Answer fools according to their folly, or they will be wise in their own eyes" (Prov. 26:5). These seem like contradictory statements. The wisdom is found in applying each to the appropriate situation.

We need to do the same for our bodies—apply different health practices to different situations. Our bodies, our minds, and our spirits need different things at different times. And certainly what we need may not be the same as what someone else needs. Instead of buying into the idea that everyone should be eating and exercising in the same way at all times, we can use our wisdom to find out what is right for us.

Take a breath and ask yourself what your body, mind, and spirit need in this moment. You might need some movement to energize you. You might need solitude or quiet. You might need something sweet or something chewy or crunchy. You might not hear a clear response, but starting to ask the question will tune your ear to your inner wisdom.

Holy Sophia, God of Wisdom, forgive me
for being rigid with the rules I apply to my
health. Help me to grow in wisdom and to
listen to what my body, mind, and spirit need
in each moment. Give me the clarity of mind
and the motivation to take care of myself
in whatever way is right for me. Amen.

Make Peace with Your Body

The wisdom from above is first pure, then peaceable, gentle, willing to yield, full of mercy and good fruits, without a trace of partiality or hypocrisy. And the fruit of righteousness is sown in peace for those who make peace.

—James 3:17-18

saw an earnest therapist once who told me to go home, take off all my clothes, stand in front of the mirror, and say to myself, "You are beautiful." I will be honest and say I didn't do it. But I appreciated her effort. Making peace with our bodies is more than standing in front of the mirror and reciting affirmations to ourselves—though it doesn't hurt to try! But I do think we can consider ways to be gentler with ourselves. We need to work at quieting the voices that bubble up with ugly, nasty words and make way for mercy. This is a spiritual practice, emphasis on the word *practice*. Each time unkind thoughts emerge, take a big deep breath and tell that voice "No." You may not know what to say next. You may not be able to utter something kind in return, but at least you can say no to the lie. Each time you find yourself disgusted with your belly or your double chin, place your warm hands on that place and pray over it. Ask God to bless it. Each time you want to curse your back or your knees for aching, be gentle with them instead. Offer them ice or heat. Take some pain reliever with water as if it were a sacrament.

One of the best steps toward making peace with your body is to buy clothes that fit your body right now. Buy something that is comfortable and that makes you feel good. And then get rid of those pieces hanging in your closet that pass judgment on you every time you go to get dressed. As writer Anne Lamott so perfectly observes, "The world is too hard as it is, without letting your pants have an opinion on how you are doing." [1] It is so much easier to be peaceful when you can fully move your arms and you aren't uncomfortable sitting in pants that are too tight. Make peace with your body, and you will reap a harvest of comfort and joy.

God of peace, I have been at war with my body for so long. Forgive me for the ways I have been downright mean to my body. Help me to make peace with the parts of me that feel hard to love. Show me ways to be gentle with myself. Amen.

Spiritual Health Is Health Too

While physical training is of some value, godliness is valuable in every way, holding promise for both the present life and the life to come.

—1 Timothy 4:8

When we think of someone who is a "health nut," what image comes to mind? Many of us imagine someone who puts a great deal of care into what they eat and into how they exercise, maybe a vegan yogi. It's interesting that we don't immediately think of someone who prioritizes rest, emotional care, and prayer. We don't always equate maintaining stable relationships and carving out time for study or for regular worship as "health" activities. Nutrition and fitness are certainly two aspects of our health, but wholistic health is so much more than that! We become so focused on our physical health that we forget how important our spiritual health is.

The writer of First Timothy reminds us of this truth in our scripture passage for today. Training our bodies is good, but godliness is even more valuable. Physical training is helpful in this life; spiritual training is eternal. However, when we are stuck in a diet-culture mindset, it's hard to even consider this. Diet culture wants everything to be about thinness and rigid adherence to its rules. Under diet culture, criticizing and discriminating against fat people are seen as promoting health. Many times people make judgmental comments about someone's body or their eating under the guise of being concerned for their health. This mentality ignores mental and spiritual health (apart from being a terrible thing to do). Cruel words, discriminatory behaviors, and structural inequalities wound people in emotional and spiritual ways. Ironically, weight stigma has been shown time and again to result in a decrease of health behaviors across the board.[2] Weight stigma not only harms our mental and spiritual health but also decreases all the other physically oriented health behaviors that it was supposed to encourage.

To heal from diet culture, we need to prioritize our spiritual health. Immersing ourselves in scripture, prayer, worship, and Christian fellowship gives us the strength and support to live a countercultural, body-positive life. In our spiritual life, we lean into our inherent value as children of God, as opposed to people who are valued by the shape of their bodies.

Physical training is of some value. Exercise and nutrition are important. Going to the doctor and following medical advice is good. There is no shame in taking medication. These are all good things. But don't throw the baby out with the bathwater. Our spiritual lives are valuable in every way. Drawing near to God gives us the promise of rich life here and now and also in eternity. Do not lose sight of the fact that spiritual health is health too.

Great Physician, help me to remember that I am more than a mass of cells and tissue. Remind me that you breathed your Spirit into my entire being. Thank you for all the incredible medical advances that you have inspired and sustained. Help me to tend not only to my body but also to my spirit. Amen.

You Are Not Alone

Encourage one another and build up each other, as indeed you are doing.

—1 Thessalonians 5:11

Have you ever wondered how a tiny seedling on the forest floor could get enough sunlight to grow into a huge tree? Suzanne Simard is a scientist who studies the forest. Her groundbreaking work has discovered that the trees, fungi, animals, and plants of the forest work together collaboratively, more like one big organism, rather than as separate entities.[3] Our modern world is shaped by the ideas of Darwin, capitalism, and patriarchy. These dominant forces teach us that we have to compete to survive in this world. But the wisdom of the forest shows us that to thrive and flourish, collaboration and cooperation are more valuable than competition.

The society around us operates in a top-down model. Success is defined by climbing to the top of the ladder, being better, and winning. But the forest—and Christ—offers us a different way, a way of community, mutual love, and respect. This way lifts all of us instead of creating a hierarchy where some have greater value and others less. In the Gospel of Luke, when the disciples are arguing over which of them is the greatest, Christ responds by saying, "The greatest among you must become like the youngest and the leader like one who serves" (22:26). Jesus tells them their argument is completely missing the point. No one is the greatest; we should all serve one another. In fact, we need one another to thrive in the way God desires for us.

Diet culture tells us the greatest among us are thin and align with normative beauty standards. This causes us to compare ourselves to one another and to compete for attention and affirmation. We see images all around us that make us feel less than. We hear the praise heaped on those who lose weight and the critical comments and glances when weight is gained. To let go of the diet-culture mindset, we need to listen to the teaching of the forest. We need to lean on one another and lift one another in a life-giving web of body-positive community.

To thrive, we need to encourage and build up one another. Embracing a body-positive mentality and lifestyle requires paddling upstream against a world that says our bodies are problems that need to be solved. When we are paddling upstream, it is highly advantageous to have several others in the canoe paddling with us. We can start by creating a community of like-minded people around us and disengaging with conversations about dieting and weight loss. It may be difficult to find people in your particular area, but you can always find online community. You can also read books, listen to podcasts, and follow social media accounts that support a body-positive ideology. As you share your journey with others, you may find that some will join you along the way.

God of relationship, I know I can't practice body positivity on my own. Forgive me for competing with my sisters and comparing myself to other women. Shift my mindset from competition to collaboration. Help me to find my community and to build up and encourage everyone I come into contact with. Amen.

Sunday

Creating Body-Positive Icons

Christian iconography has played an important role in the spiritual lives of Christians for hundreds of years. From the earliest days of Christianity, artists have created beautiful, gilded portrayals of Jesus, Mary, and various saints that draw our eyes and create a visual field for gazing into the heart of God. The rich symbols of Christian icons provide a different sort of language for learning about the Spirit and the stories of our faith. Religious icons are meant to inspire us and remind us of the spark of the Spirit that lives within all of us. These sacred visual images create space for our eyes to linger, for symbols to soak into our unconscious, subtly forming our inner world.

However, while Christian icons used art as a way of highlighting the beauty and mystery of our faith, our modern world's icons are those who meet the standards of the thin, White beauty ideal. Magazines, social media, and ubiquitous advertisements communicate a clear image that thin bodies are the best bodies. Our constant exposure to these images is harming our level of satisfaction with our bodies and our ability to see the beauty in the diverse array of bodies around us. A study in 2016 surveyed 230 college-aged women about their exposure to fashion magazines, and it found that higher exposure to fashion magazines significantly increased levels of body dissatisfaction and harmed psychological health.[4] What we are visually exposed to influences what we believe, how we feel, and how we behave.

Short of moving to a deserted island, completely escaping the visual images of diet culture and the thin ideal is practically impossible. However, we do have the power to infuse our visual life with as many beautifully diverse body icons as we can. Dr. Michelle Lelwica writes this: "The Religion of Thinness relies on the suppression of diversity. Alternative visions of beauty are excluded. Perhaps if we encountered glamorous likenesses of other body types more often, we would be able to embrace the slender bodies as just one possibility among many." [5] We can be intentional about adding body-positive icons into our visual world. We can seek out social media accounts that celebrate women in bigger bodies, we can support clothing brands that hire diverse models for their advertising, and we can watch movies and TV shows that feature women of different body sizes and abilities in prominent roles. The following activity is intended to help you create a new body-positive icon to use in your spiritual practice.

Materials

- Picture of yourself or of a woman whose body size and shape you would like to honor (I've personally found using a picture of myself for this activity to be powerful.)
- Small canvas or sturdy card stock
- Tracing paper
- Permanent marker
- Pencil
- Glue stick
- Scissors
- Markers or paints for embellishing
- Special papers and/or magazines for collage
- Gold paint (I use a gouache, but craft paint or acrylic will work just fine.)
- *(Optional)* Water-based glue or sealant (for example, Mod Podge)

Instructions

- Lay the tracing paper over your picture, and use a permanent marker to trace the important features of the body in the picture.
- Cut out the tracing paper image, or glue the whole page to your canvas or card stock.
- Use markers and paints to add color and detail to your image. You can leave it as a simple outline or add as much detail as you want.
- Use your papers and magazines to add embellishments around the body. In Christian iconography, the use of symbolic objects creates added layers of meaning. You may choose to research some of these traditional symbols and use them in your icon. I also like to use traditional symbols associated with plants and flowers. For instance, in the Victorian era, black-eyed Susans symbolized justice and calla lilies symbolized beauty. Adding them both to an image might represent beauty justice. There are many different cultural traditions that give particular symbolic meanings to plants, animals, and other items. Research your own cultural background to see what you can find. Add whatever images speak to you.
- (This is my favorite part!) Use your pencil to lightly draw a circle around the head of your body. You can use something circular to trace or draw the circle freehand. Then use your gold paint to fill in the circle, creating a gilded halo. You can use the gold paint to highlight or embellish any part of your image.
- Use markers, paint, or a permanent marker to add meaningful words to your icon. You can add scripture, poetry, song lyrics, a line from a personal letter, or anything else that speaks to you. You can also leave your icon as is with no words.
- *(Optional)* To preserve your icon, consider applying a water-based glue or sealant or a clear-coat acrylic spray.

Blessing

Place your finished icon in a meaningful space. You can place some small sacred objects in front of it, such as prayer beads, special stones, or flowers. Place a candle in front of the icon and light it. Pray this blessing:

> God of beauty, I dedicate this icon to you. May it draw me inward to the place where you dwell inside me. May it remind me of the goodness you have created in my body and in all bodies. May it help to change my vision so that I can see the beauty in bodies of all shapes, sizes, and abilities. Amen.

WEEK

three

Eating for the Glory of God

Whether you eat or drink or whatever you do, do everything for the glory of God.

—1 Corinthians 10:31

Every morning, I ask my four-year-old what he would like for breakfast, and every morning he spends a great deal of time deliberating. This morning he ran through the options aloud, listing them one by one. "Let's see . . . bagel? No. Eggs? No. Yogurt? No." And then his eye caught a ripe, juicy pear perched on the windowsill behind the sink. His eyes widened, and he said, "Pear! With a side of Captain Crunch and milk please." I sliced the pear for him and watched him dig in. He bit into that pear with his eyes closed, juice dribbling down his chin. With his mouth full he said, "I weely wuv pears."

I immediately had this thought: *This kid is eating for the glory of God.* He listened to his body, thought about what he was hungry for, and made his choice. Eating for the glory of God doesn't require eating some sort of "perfect" or "clean" diet. Those things don't exist anyway. But choosing what is right for our bodies in the moment—what will make us feel good and give us the strength and energy to live life to the fullest—glorifies God.

Dietitians and authors Evelyn Tribole and Elyse Resch have pioneered the Intuitive Eating model for breaking free from the trap of dieting. Intuitive Eating has ten principles, and addressing nutrition and health doesn't come until the very last one. Tribole and Resch write that "if a healthy relationship with food is not in place, it's difficult to truly pursue healthy eating. If you've been a chronic dieter or immersed in some form of diet culture, the best nutrition guidelines can still be embraced like a diet."[1] We can get so caught up in eating "healthy" that our stress about what to eat actually becomes more of a health problem than any "unhealthy" food we may have eaten to begin with. Nutrition is important, but good nutrition does not require perfection. Tuning into our mental health and what gives us pleasure are also important parts of our overall health.

Whatever food you find yourself drawn to today, eat it for the glory of God. Close your eyes and let the pear juice drip down your chin. Enjoy the crunch of that cereal. Notice the earthy flavor of the salad. Let the fudge melt on your tongue. And give thanks to God for all these blessings.

> Nourishing God, thank you for creating such a diverse array of food for me to choose from. Help me to embrace nutrition gently, without gripping too tightly to hard-and-fast rules. Help me to choose food that will nourish me well and bring me joy. Amen.

Body Diversity
Is Beautiful

Just as the body is one and has many members, and all the members of the body, though many, are one body, so it is with Christ. For in the one Spirit we were all baptized into one body—Jews or Greeks, slaves or free—and we were all made to drink of one Spirit.

—1 Corinthians 12:12-13

Growing up I loved the Muppets. Who am I kidding—I still love the Muppets! One of the things I love about those crazy furry friends is that they represent a broad range of diversity in the Muppet world. A pig can marry a frog. A bear can pal around with a dog. There's even Gonzo, whose species we are still unsure of. The Muppets don't always get along, but they stick together and have lots of fun adventures. I particularly love the character of Miss Piggy. She is a glamorous, plus-sized female who knows what she wants and isn't afraid to go out there and get it.

Diversity is a key part of what it means to become whole as a community. Paul reminds us of the beautiful diversity that exists among God's children. We are not all meant to look the same or have the same gifts, but when we come together in the name of Love, we become one beautiful body—the body of Christ. The dominant narrative in our society is that only certain types of bodies are beautiful. This beauty standard puts cisgendered, White, thin bodies on a pedestal and pushes all others to the margins. Diet culture tells us we don't get to have love or achieve our dreams or enjoy the everyday treasures of life unless we look a certain way. But our Christian story paints a different picture. In Christ there is space to celebrate all forms of beauty. The circle is wide enough for all bodies to join. Even if we're a little different, like Gonzo, or big and bold, like Miss Piggy. It also means that we are all lovable and deserve full, adventurous lives. Just like that ragtag group of Muppets.

Know that no matter what type of body you have, you do belong. And when you start to believe that, look around you and see if you can spot anyone on the outskirts who feels like they don't get to join. When you spot them, grab their hand and pull them in. The body of Christ needs as much diversity as it can get.

Creator God, you made each of us so unique. Teach my eyes to see the beauty in all bodies and in all people. Help me to create spaces where everyone feels they belong. Forgive me for the ways I have judged myself and others. Inspire me to love those who are different from me. Amen.

Bread of Life

"The bread of God is that which comes down from heaven and gives life to the world." They said to him, "Sir, give us this bread always." Jesus said to them, "I am the bread of life. Whoever comes to me will never be hungry, and whoever believes in me will never be thirsty."

—John 6:33-35

There is something so wonderful about Jesus calling himself bread. If Jesus were to walk among us today, I can imagine him picking up the latest low-carb diet book and throwing it across the room. He'd gather us around him and say, "Listen, I am the bread of life. Would the Savior of all creation name himself after a food that is supposedly bad for you? No. No, I wouldn't. Pass the olive oil."

Carbohydrates are a fundamental source of energy for our bodies. They are essential for our lives, yet even this basic macronutrient has been so demonized by diet culture that we are afraid to eat the very food that Jesus used as a powerful symbol. The irony is that the more we restrict ourselves from various types of foods, the more we crave those foods and the more we are likely to binge or feel out of control around them. However, if we give ourselves permission to eat whatever we want, whenever we want, in whatever quantity feels right, then the "off-limits" foods lose their power. Letting go of a restrictive mindset around food is one of the first stages of intuitive eating.

When you begin practicing intuitive eating, your body may need some time to register that you have full permission to eat whatever and however much you want. And this may result in eating a lot of your favorite foods for a while. That is OK. There is nothing "bad" about the foods you love and crave. You may feel like you will never stop eating a particular food, but eventually your body stops craving whole boxes of oatmeal cream pies. Trust me. I have a whole box of them in my pantry, and it has lived there for several weeks. That would NEVER have happened when I was in diet-culture mindset. I was the girl with fistfuls of Starbursts in her pocket, trying to discretely unwrap and chew them in serious work meetings without being noticed. Now I can eat Starbursts whenever I want, and I don't feel ruled by them. There are definitely times when I crave them, but when I do, I just eat them and move on. The craving doesn't consume my life, nor does a sense of shame or guilt for having satisfied my desire.

Jesus wants this kind of freedom for us. He says to us, "Come to me and you will never be hungry. Let go of all those ways you are trying to control your body and rest in me. I will give you your life back." In Christ we can trade restriction for abundance. Diet culture makes us feel like we must live a life of scarcity. It tells us we must live deprived. But God created an abundant world for us to cherish and be fed by. Christ chose food—bread, even—as the symbol for the spiritual fulfillment to be found in Jesus. God does not want deprivation or scarcity for us, physically or spiritually. When we let go of the scarcity mindset, we can take all the energy and space that was sucked up by our hyper-focus on food, exercise, and weight and turn that focus on deepening our spiritual life and living in creative, flourishing joy.

Bread of life, thank you for being my source of sustenance. Thank you for providing abundant ways to nourish my body, mind, and spirit. Help me to remember that there is enough. Free me from the cycle of restriction and feeling out of control. Amen.

God Had a Body

The Word became flesh and lived among us, and we have seen his glory, the glory as of a father's only son, full of grace and truth.

—John 1:14

Christians believe God walked around on the earth in flesh and blood in the person of Jesus. What an amazing thought! That means God meets us right here in our fleshy, bloody, sometimes stinky bodies. It means God—through Jesus—stubbed his toe and ate until his belly was about to burst and got stuck in the rain and felt grass under his feet and warm sun on his skin and had morning breath. God knows what it is like to be in a body, to feel its wonder and its limitations. It means that the human body is an integral part of God's salvation plan.

Christianity, especially the White, Western version, tends to be thought oriented. We listen to sermons, study the Bible, and speak of our faith as a sort of mental exercise. The desires or needs of the body are treated as something to overcome. Sexual urges, hungers, passions, and pleasures are all things to fear and contain. If God had a body, why do we think we need to transcend ours to get to God? Why do we get so stuck in our heads or believe we need to silence our bodies in order to be "spiritual"? God created us with these bodies and gave them wisdom. Our bodies are the only place we have to encounter God. They are not separate from our spirit, but rather the material embodiment of God's image.

Every atom holds the Divine breath. And because God had a body, we know that God understands the body frustrations that we face. God has empathy and compassion for us when we bump against the limits of our body. Jesus probably never went on a diet, but Jesus can understand our temptation to join the dominant cultural narrative that pushes us to do so.

God became human so that we could be saved, and the only way to be saved is by being fully human like Jesus was human. We can work out our salvation with fear and trembling by leaning into our humanity. We can look for ways to live incarnationally, seeing humanity and all of creation as the place where the Divine meets the mortal. Living incarnationally means paying close attention. It means looking for God in all the creation around us, including in our bodies.

Slow down. Go outside and smell the air after a rain shower. Feel the cool water surrounding you in the pool. Recognize the beauty in the sound of your friend's laughter. God is right there waiting for you. God meets you in your body, and that's very good news.

God, you became human just like me. Thank you for loving me so much that you took on a physical body and walked the earth, even though that meant taking on pain and suffering. My body is the place where I experience your love and the instrument through which I share your love with others. Allow me to notice the ways you are in each scent, each touch, each taste, each sound. Amen.

You Don't Need to Be Perfect

He said to me, "My grace is sufficient for you, for power is made perfect in weakness." So, I will boast all the more gladly of my weaknesses, so that the power of Christ may dwell in me.

—2 Corinthians 12:9

On a brisk, sunny October morning in Chicago, I hopped on an L train and headed to Grant Park to support my friend who was running the Chicago Marathon for the first time. I had never witnessed such an event, and I was swept away by the energy of the crowd and the excitement in the air. Each year the city comes out in full support of the marathon runners, with each neighborhood adding its own flair. There are bands playing on street corners, Chinese dragons dancing in Chinatown, and crowds covering overpasses with signs and streamers. I was impressed. And even though I had always hated running, I decided then and there that I would run a marathon.

Most people would work their way up to such an event. Starting with a good number of 5K races, maybe work up to a 10K. That's what normal people would do. But I struggle with an all-or-nothing attitude. I need to do something all the way or not at all. So if I was going to run, then I was going to RUN. My first race ever was a half marathon, and my second race was a marathon. It was an incredible experience, and I'm glad I did it. But after that race, I felt like I couldn't stop. I couldn't mix it up. I was a runner now, and being a runner meant I had to get in twenty-five miles a week whether I wanted to or not. With this all-or-nothing, perfectionist mindset, I eventually ended up with knee pain and a miserable attitude. I was running, but I was grumpy about it. I dreaded it. And I ended up quitting for several years.

Striving to be perfect at something usually ends this way. When I couldn't keep up the perfectionist pace with my running, I felt guilty and weak. That sense of shame led me to abandon something that could have continued to be life-giving if I had approached it with flexibility and grace. Diet culture thrives on perfectionism. It tells us we must eat perfectly, exercise perfectly, strive for the "perfect" body. Perfectionism is another way diet culture reels us in and keeps us stuck. It dangles false promises in front of us, telling us that if we could just execute the next diet with perfection, we could have it all.

We know humans are not perfect, but that does not stop us from trying to be the first one to get there. Whether it is our work, our parenting, our eating, our pursuit of health, or even our faith, when we demand perfection from ourselves, we inevitably end up in a pile of disappointment, shame, and self-loathing. When that happens, the shame can paralyze us and keep us from staying engaged in our lives.

The good news is we don't have to be perfect. God knows we aren't perfect and loves us anyway. God's grace is sufficient and never-ending. When we stop trying to be perfect and start embracing the power of Christ that lives within us, we can engage our bodies with wisdom and flexibility. We can enjoy running and take a break when we need it. We can ease into practices or routines and embrace the learning curve. When we feel the pull to perfectionist thinking, we can remind ourselves that power is made perfect in weakness and grace is sufficient for all the times we turn out to be mortal.

Perfect God, forgive me for trying to
be perfect. I am grateful for your grace.
Help me to be flexible and to offer
myself the same grace that you
give to me over and over again. Amen.

Inherited Diet Culture

May you be made strong with all the strength that comes from his glorious power, so that you may have all endurance and patience, joyfully giving thanks to the Father, who has enabled you to share in the inheritance of the saints in the light.

—Colossians 1:11-12

My mom has been on a diet for as long as I can remember. She has lost and gained the same thirty to fifty pounds more times than I can count. My mom's discomfort with her body's size and shape formed a constant refrain during my childhood that brought with it endless grilled chicken breasts, Snackwell's cookies, speed-walking through the neighborhood, and *Sweatin' to the Oldies* sessions in the living room. Weight Watchers was a regular presence in my childhood home. I am now forty-two, and I can count on one hand the times I have seen my mother in a swimsuit.

My mom's relationships with her body, with food, and with exercise were the soundtrack to my childhood and adolescence. She projected some of that onto me, warning that I needed to be careful so that I didn't turn into a "chubby teen." But even if she had never directly talked about my body, her actions implied that being thin was the goal.

I write this with great compassion and love for my mom and for all of us who are barraged with the message that thin is the highest ideal. My mom was doing what her doctors and Oprah and every women's maga-zine were screaming at her to do. Her dieting was her attempt at taking care of herself, and she thought that what she was projecting onto me was out of care for my health and happiness. Yet those messages seeped into my psyche and left a mark that led to years of hating my body and doing everything I could to shrink it.

The struggles of our parents are passed down to us, but we don't have to live into that inheritance. Christ offers us a different inheritance, one of freedom and light. Today's scripture passage is from the opening of Paul's letter to the Colossians. He reminds them of who they belong to and prays for God to give them strength, endurance, and patience. We need that strength and patience to walk a different path than the one many of our mothers and mother-figures walked before us. Going against the messages about our bodies that we were taught, implicitly and explicitly, can be a struggle. It can feel counterintuitive and even like we are doing something wrong. But we find strength in our inherited identity as children of God. When we choose to say no to diet culture, we are free to say yes to all the good things God has in store for us.

> God of my foremothers, so many generations of women have gone before me who have struggled with their body image. And their beliefs were passed down to me. God, strengthen me as I turn away from diet culture and turn toward you. Help me to live into your inheritance of light and to love you and love my body. Amen.

Sunday

Spiritual Body Mapping

ody mapping is an activity that creates a visual representation of how you perceive and experience your body. Often it is used to help process emotions or to build more body awareness. It is even used for developing embodied artistic expression, such as in theater or dance. Here you will use body mapping to explore the connection between your body and spirit. Hopefully this practice will bring greater awareness to how you experience God in and through your body. In addition, this practice is intended to create space for you to bask in God's healing love.

Supplies

- Paper
- Pen or pencil
- Markers/crayons/colored pencils
- Any other desired art supplies

Directions

1. Create an outline of your body.

   Option 1: If you have the space, paper, and a trusted friend, you can outline your entire body. If you choose this route, lie down and position yourself comfortably on the paper, and ask your friend to draw an outline of you.

Option 2: You can draw an outline freehand. This does not need to be an accurate or proportional depiction of your silhouette. In fact, you can use the outline to depict parts of your body as you perceive them. For instance, if you feel like you live too much in your head, you could exaggerate the size of your head.

Option 3: If drawing the outline feels like a barrier, find a simple body outline online. Feel free to use a marker or pen to alter its shape to suit you.

2. Choose a color for each of the following prompts. Then add shapes, symbols, images, or textures that represent your response to the prompt.

    a. Consider the part or parts of your body you have the hardest time loving. Mark these areas on your map with colors, shapes, or symbols that represent your feelings.

    b. Consider the part or parts of your body that you love. Mark these areas in a way that represents your feelings.

    c. Choose a color that represents God's presence. Close your eyes, take a deep breath, and remember the last time you sensed God's presence. Mark the sensations you remember feeling on your map.

    d. Choose a color that represents God's love. Use that color to circle any area on your map that you marked in the first prompt.

    e. Circle your entire body with the color you used for God's love.

3. Take some time to sit with your map. What words, shapes, or images come to you? You can write, draw, or add words and images cut from magazines to your body map.

4. When you have finished adorning your body map, place one hand on the map and one hand on your own body. If you can

comfortably reach the part of your body you have the most difficult time loving, place a hand on that part of yourself. If not, rest your hand on your belly or chest. Take three deep breaths.

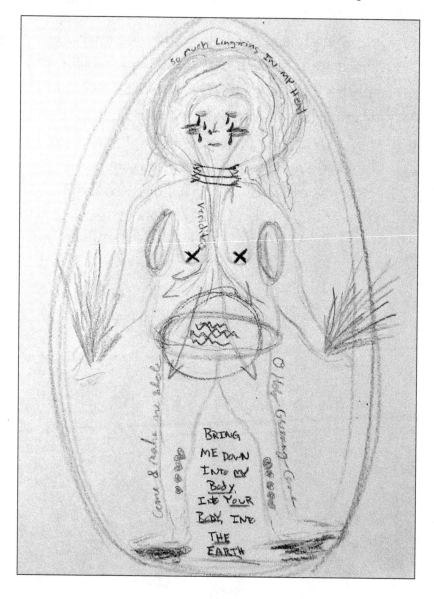

Pray the following prayer:

God, sometimes I struggle with loving my body.
There are parts of it that I wish were smaller,
smoother, tighter, more proportionate. Help me
to see myself as you see me. Help me to see
that you love every inch of me, even the squishy/
wrinkly/pointy/graying/(fill in the blank) parts.
Heal my relationship with my body so that I
can be free to fully experience your presence
and the joy you intend for me. Amen.

WEEK

four

What Will We Pass Down?

"If any of you cause on of these little ones who believe in me to sin, it would be better for you if a great millstone were fastened around your neck and you were drowned in the depth of the sea."

—Matthew 18:6

tossed my wiggly, giggly five-year-old girl onto the couch and tumbled down onto the cushions after her, initiating a session of what she and her brother affectionately call "Wraaaastle time!" This involves a great deal of tickling, tossing kids into the air, and getting squished with lots of pillows from all sides. Somewhere in the tangle of elbows and knees, my T-shirt slipped up around my neck, exposing my belly. My belly is hands down my least favorite part of my body. I am still on a journey of figuring out how to love it well. And there I was, upside down on a couch with my most vulnerable body part exposed. My five-year-old jumped at the chance to get close to this part of my body she rarely sees, and she laid her head down on it. She started to massage my soft, round stomach with her little fingers, chanting, "Squishy belly! Squishy belly!"

In that moment, the air was sucked right out of me. I felt as though my daughter had found the one open wound in my soul and poked her finger directly into it. I immediately wanted to pull my shirt down and correct her for talking about my body that way. But I paused. I knew she

wasn't criticizing me. That was my own projection. Instead of responding with my initial feelings, I took a couple breaths. My deep breathing
slowed our play, and my daughter melted into a snuggle, head still pressed
to my belly. She ran her little hand along my side and said, "Mommy, I
love your squishy belly."

As our daughters, granddaughters, nieces, friends, and neighbors grow
up, they are soaking in all the ways we talk about and treat our bodies.
How easily we create stumbling blocks for the next generation by criticizing ourselves aloud, by engaging in restrictive eating or obsessive exercise,
and by talking about food, exercise, and bodies in ways that perpetuate
diet culture. When we judge ourselves and others, we must remember that
others may be watching and listening. Let us be mindful of what we pass
on to those who are growing up around us. And if we watch and listen to
them, they may just show us how to love our squishy bellies.

God, the perfect Parent, forgive me for the
ways I have passed on harmful beliefs and
behaviors to the next generation. Help me
to pause and breathe when I feel triggered
by diet culture so that I can pass on love and
wisdom instead. Help me to love my body so
that those around me will love theirs too. Amen.

Living in a
Resurrection Body

Your dead shall live; their corpses shall rise.
   Those who dwell in the dust will awake and shout for joy!
For your dew is a radiant dew,
   and the earth will give birth to those long dead.

—Isaiah 26:19

One year my mother and her husband planned a family cruise to the Caribbean. There would be sun and water and piña coladas and strange games that involved seeing who could shove fruit into their bathing suit the fastest. I had never been on a cruise or to the Caribbean, so I was excited. But I was also anxious. I knew that trip would involve a lot of time in a bathing suit. So I ramped up my running and kicked my food restriction into high gear. When I went on that cruise, I was probably the smallest I have ever been in my life. Yet every moment of the trip I worried about my body. Every day I fretted about what I looked like in my bathing suit. I worried about what I was eating. I counted the calories in the piña coladas. I found the fitness center on the boat and made myself exercise. Yes, the cruise included some lovely moments, but my prevailing memory is how I felt about my body. People were enjoying themselves all around me, but I could only focus on berating myself for how I looked.

In many ways, internalized fat phobia and our worship of thinness cause us to miss out on life. Our hyperfocus on what our bodies look like leaves us anxious and distracted and oblivious to what is happening around us. Instead of living fully into each moment, soaking up the sunshine and relishing the cool tropical drink in our hand, we are fretting and scanning the environment, comparing ourselves to others. Life becomes limited to one interest. Diet culture forms blinders that keep our focus on our inadequacies. Our constant pursuit of the thin ideal leaves us consumed with this one desire, but we can never achieve it. We spend an enormous amount of time, energy, and mental capacity focused on weight loss, but we are still left hungry and roaming the internet or the latest diet book to find the answer to our body troubles. We miss out on all the goodness and love and creativity that we pass by on our way to the gym. What a dreary way to live.

Emerging from a diet-culture mentality can feel like coming back to life. When we are able to shed the lies of diet culture, the world seems more vibrant and inviting. We can shake off the dust of that dreary, limited life and sing for joy! God wants resurrection life for us. God wants us to rise from our body loathing and walk this radiant earth with joyful abundance. The next time you find me on a cruise, you better believe I will be enjoying myself. Never again will I let diet culture get in the way of me winning a poolside karaoke competition in my bikini. That prize is mine for the taking!

God of resurrection life, I have spent too much time living like the walking dead. Wake me up. Show me all the good things you have in store. Help me to shake off the dust and sing for joy because you have made this body and called it very good. Amen.

All Food Is Morally Neutral

Eat whatever is sold in the meat market without raising any question on the ground of conscience, for "the earth and its fullness are the Lord's." If an unbeliever invites you to a meal and you are disposed to go, eat whatever is set before you without raising any question on the ground of conscience.

—1 Corinthians 10:25-27

The language we use to talk about food is frequently dripping with moral overtones. Commercials feature women sensually biting into chocolate and calling it "sinful." After we indulge in a decadent meal, we talk about how "bad" we were and how "guilty" we feel. Days taken off from a diet are called "cheat days." We categorize food into good/bad, health food/junk food, sinful/virtuous. The binaries that these categories create are illusions. No number of calories can move a type of food from the "good" category into the "bad" category.

In this passage from First Corinthians, Paul responds to a concern in the early church in Corinth about whether they should eat meat that was used in pagan temple worship. The Corinthians were worried that because it had been used in pagan worship, eating this meat was an immoral act. They were literally worried that this food was sinful. Even in this context, when there was a pagan ritual act performed with the food, Paul writes that the Corinthians should eat it freely. Food is morally neutral. We are free to eat whatever we hunger for.

When we start to assign morality to food, we automatically create a situation in which some foods are off limits. When we label food as a vice, we create a situation where we will crave the thing we are not allowed to have. However, our body is designed to protect us against deprivation. Inevitably, we will cave to the craving because of our body's natural responses, and this creates guilt, shame, and fear of being out of control. When this happens, we blame ourselves for lack of willpower and continue to demonize the foods we are craving, when, in fact, it was our body naturally correcting from the deprivation.

Just before today's scripture passage in First Corinthians, Paul writes, "'All things are permitted,' but not all things are beneficial" (10:23). A starting point for shifting our mindset around food might be asking ourselves, *What is beneficial?* Diet culture wants us to believe that whatever makes us thin is beneficial. The truth is there are many ways food can be beneficial. What is beneficial when it comes to food involves more than just calorie count. Foods can be beneficial because they are nutritious, filling, satisfying, tasty, celebratory, sweet, savory, convenient, ceremonial, or made just for us. There are so many reasons why we eat and so many reasons to choose certain foods at certain times. May we listen to our bodies and souls and feed them whatever they crave. Everything is permissible. Everything is on the table. We can choose what is beneficial for us in each moment.

God of all good things, thank you for providing such a diversity of food for me to choose from. Help me to trust that all foods are permissible so that I can be free to choose what is right for me in the moment. Free me from any guilt or fear I have about what or how much I choose to eat. Amen.

Salvation Came Through a Woman's Body

The angel said to her, "Do not be afraid, Mary, for you have found favor with God. And now, you will conceive in your womb and bear a son, and you will name him Jesus."
—Luke 1:30-31

The mother of God probably had stretch marks. There aren't many of us who make it through growing a human inside us who don't. Mary's breasts grew heavy and firm with milk, just like any breastfeeding mom. It's likely she had swollen feet and couldn't get comfortable at night and woke up with heartburn after she finally fell asleep. I don't know if the angel's promises about how awesome Jesus was going to be were any consolation for the way he kicked her right in the ribs on a regular basis. I won't even go into what it must have been like giving birth without modern medicine and with farm animals looking on. Carrying the Son of God in her womb was no easy task, and it surely took a physical toll. I'm sure that after she birthed and weened the Christ child, her breasts lost some of their fullness and her tummy softened. Maybe her hair changed texture, or her feet grew a half size bigger.

The church has historically not been kind to women's bodies. Our bodies have been blamed for everything from the poor behavior of lustful men to the fall of all humankind with Eve's forbidden fruit. Our bodies have been treated as property, as sexual objects, as weaker and inferior. But let us not forget that salvation came to us through a woman's body. It is easy to think of Jesus as if he just appeared at the age of thirty, fully grown and ready to make miracles happen. Yet, if there was no Mary, then there would be no Jesus. Her body was the starting place for God's human life.

Mary's body was a mother's body—soft and stretched, growing and changing each day. When we are faced with messages that tell us our bodies are not good enough, we can remember Mary. Mary's body allowed her to birth the Christ child—not in spite of her womanhood but because of it. We can relate to Mary whether we've given birth, desperately wish to give birth, or never want to carry a child in our womb. Regardless, our bodies are a source of creative wonder. Our bodies are not something to be covered up or kept quietly off to the side. They are powerful and Spirit-filled, and we should honor them as such.

Jesus, you know what it is like to live in a body. You know what it's like to have a mother who loved you with her whole body, who let her body be changed and reshaped so that you could be born. Help me to love my body for all that it can create and birth into the world. Help me to love the ways my body shows its power and creativity. Amen.

There Is a Body for Every Season

For everything there is a season and a time for every matter under heaven.

—Ecclesiastes 3:1

Our bodies are temples for the Holy Spirit. In an actual temple or church, the space is decorated and used according to the occasion. During Lent, many sanctuaries are decked in purple. We sing penitential songs and talk of mortality and sin. On Good Friday, the altar will be stripped, and black fabric will be draped over crosses. The lights will be dim and somber, and grief-laden music will be sung. On Easter morning, the sanctuary will be clothed in bright white and gold. There may be trumpets or loud joyful hymns. The scent of lilies will fill the space.

This diversity is true for your bodily temple as well. Honoring and respecting your body will look different from one day to the next. On days when you are feeling sluggish and down, you may need extra rest and gentle movement. When you have days filled with anxiety and stress, you may want to focus on your breathing or try quiet spiritual practices. Some days you have the energy and excitement to climb mountains, and some days you may be a little lonely and need to call a friend.

The way you tend to your temple is specific to you. What works for one person in one circumstance may not work for someone else in the same situation. When I am anxious, I know a vigorous workout will shift my mood and soothe my spirit. A friend of mine needs stillness and solitude when she is anxious. What your temple needs will also be different in different seasons or periods of your life. For instance, after a busy, decadent Christmas season, I crave simplicity. I want quiet and routine. I want to be outdoors and to do yoga. But in slower periods of life, I know I need to seek time with friends. Interestingly, I find that slower periods of life offer a space for me to try new things and be adventurous.

Diet culture tells us we need to adhere to rigid meal plans and workouts no matter what our bodies tell us they need. Diet culture wants us to ignore our hunger cues or the signs that our bodies need rest. Diet culture doesn't allow us to honor the sacredness and uniqueness of our bodies, and we may forget that the Holy Spirit resides within us. So how do we overcome the lies that diet culture tells us? We can consider what our temple needs in each moment and allow our bodies to need different things in different seasons. And we can honor our bodies as temples by adorning them and engaging with them in different ways in different seasons. May we remember that our bodies are homes for the Holy Spirit.

Holy God, help me to understand my body as a sacred space. Open my ears to listen for what it needs in each moment. I want to honor this body by being attuned to its needs. Help me to take good care of this temple. Amen.

All Bodies Are
Good Bodies

God created humans in his image,
in the image of God he created them; . . .
God saw everything that he had made, and indeed, it was
very good.

—Genesis 1:27, 31

For thousands of years people have tried to make sense of what it means to be created in God's image. Some, like Augustine in the fourth century, propose it is our rationality or ability to choose that is made in God's image.[1] Others, like Martin Luther, have said it is our dominion over the rest of creation that represents the Divine image.[2] Still others, such as Karl Barth, have said it's our relational nature that bears God's image.[3] But all these ideas separate our physical bodies from some thinking, feeling, or spiritual part of us. Genesis doesn't say, "God created the invisible soul part of humans in God's own image" or "God created the smart part of humans in God's own image." It says God created humans in God's own image.

I believe our whole selves are made in God's image, and our bodies are part of the deal. This dualistic idea that our bodies are somehow not connected to the spiritual aspects of our being is a farce. We are not robots that God inserted an *imago dei* microchip into that will somehow upload its contents to heaven at the moment of our death. Our bodies are not shells. Every cell is infused with the spark of the Divine.

Many of us have grown up being taught that the spirit and the body are separate and that the spirit is the superior part. We were told the body is the part that gets us into trouble. The body is full of lust and sensuality and hunger, and the way to be a good Christian is to dominate all the body's desires. The results of this teaching have been particularly hard on women, who have been blamed for centuries for the hungers of Eve in the Garden. In the second century, Tertullian even called women "the devil's gateway" and blamed women for Christ's death all because of Eve's hunger.[4] As women, we have been taught to quiet our desires, suppress our sexuality and our physical hunger, and to cover up or feel ashamed of our bodies. For thousands of years our reproductive systems and menstrual cycles have been labeled dirty and shameful. It is time to say no to all that. It is time to reclaim our created goodness. It is time to say, "God created this body and called it good." It is time to reject the idea that hunger is evil. And it is time to start honoring the sacredness held in our bodies.

Let yourself feel the presence of the holy in your belly. If you menstruate, recognize the creative power of the Divine in your monthly cycle. Listen to the ways the Spirit speaks to you through goose bumps and shivers of sensation that travel all over the surface of your skin. And let your hungers teach you what God desires for you.

Creator God, help me to remember that you created me and called me good. Quiet the voices around me that try to tell me this body is something to be ashamed of. Help me to recognize the ways you are present in my body and to listen to the wisdom you have implanted in every cell of my being. Amen.

Sunday

Watch Your Words

The world around us operates under the false assumption that being thin is the ultimate goal and that everyone is aiming for that goal. Because of this, the language we hear every day can be intensely anti-fat biased. This language becomes second nature to us, and we don't think twice hearing it or even using it ourselves. For example, a friend asks, "Does this outfit make me look fat?" Without missing a beat, we reassure her by saying, "No! You don't look fat!" The implied message in her question is that fat is a terrible way to look. And our answer implies our agreement. What does it feel like for someone who identifies herself as fat to hear this dialogue?

Our language also can hold diet-culture messaging that keeps the lies about our bodies, food, and exercise alive in us. Without thinking, we talk about feeling guilty for things we eat or having to "earn" our dessert through exercise. Our words are powerful. They can hurt others and keep us trapped in a harmful mindset.

Here are some common examples of language that might be harmful. In the days and weeks to come, examine how you speak to yourself and others. What changes can you make?

Diet-Culture Language	Try This Instead
"I feel so fat."	Think about what you really are feeling. It might be bloated or full. You might feel insecure or in need of affirmation. You might feel sluggish. It might mean your clothes don't fit or the chair you are in is not made for you. Fat is not a feeling. Name how you are feeling, and respond to that feeling without anti-fat bias.
"Does this make me look fat?"	Ask yourself why it would be bad to look fat. It's not. If you find yourself wanting to ask this question, practice saying, "It's okay to be fat."
"This chocolate is sinful."	Remind yourself that all foods are morally neutral. You are not sinning by eating chocolate or any other food.
"I feel so guilty for eating this!"	There is no food condemnation in Christ! You are free to eat what you please. Talk back to that inner voice of guilt and shame and say, "Get behind me, Satan!"

| "I'll have to hit the gym hard to make up for all this food." | First, we don't have to govern what and how much we eat depending on how and if we exercise. Second, exercise and movement should be about loving your body and finding joy, not about punishing yourself. Enjoy whatever deliciousness you are eating. Then move your body when it feels right to do so because you want to, not because you need to compensate for a meal. |

WEEK
five

You Can Trust
Your Body

It was you who formed my inward parts;
you knit me together in my mother's womb.
I praise you, for I am fearfully and wonderfully made.
Wonderful are your works;
that I know very well.

—Psalm 139:13-14

sat across from a dear friend in a dark corner of our favorite bookish coffee shop. With a warm latte cupped in my hands, I tried out my thought experiment on her. "What would it be like if we just stopped trying to lose weight? What if we just let go of it all and ate what we wanted and exercised for fun?" We entered into one of those sitcom pauses where both conversation partners look at each other to suss out whether the other is serious, and then we broke the silence in nervous laughter. I don't remember exactly what I said next, but I'm sure it was something like, "But we could never do that, right?" Right?

But that pause—it was pregnant with something. Both of us desperately wanted freedom from the constant burden of diet culture. To live a life that was free of constantly worrying about calories or macros, a life that was not shackled to a treadmill—that sounded heavenly. But neither of us knew that diet culture was a thing, let alone that it was lying to us about the inherent worth of our bodies. We thought it was just the way the world was, the way science and medicine were, the way beauty and self-worth were. The bottom line was that we could *not* trust our bodies. If we wanted health and happiness, we could not let our bodies take the steering wheel.

But our bodies are wise. So wise. The psalmist writes that we are "fearfully and wonderfully made." God knit our very bodies together with intricate stitches and complexity. And that complexity and beauty can be trusted. We have built-in hunger cues that tell us when our bodies need food. And when we ignore these cues, our bodies are not fooled. Instead, they work to keep us from starving. Dietitians Evelyn Tribole and Elyse Resch put it this way: "Our need for food (energy) is so essential and primal that if we are not getting enough energy, our bodies naturally compensate with powerful biological and psychological mechanisms."[1] Our bodies know what they need, and when we try to restrict them, they hijack the brain and the rest of our biology to make sure our bodies can continue to function and exist.

If we truly believe we are wonderfully made, shouldn't we be able to trust in God's handiwork? I propose we stop trying to override the wisdom that God built into our bodies. Instead, let's listen to our bodies' cues and respond with deep, loving care. Let's tune our attention to the ways God speaks to us in and through the rhythms of the body. We can trust God, and we can trust our bodies.

> God, you knit my body together while I was still in my mother's womb. You made me beautiful, and you filled my body with wisdom. You made this body a survivor, and she knows how to take care of herself. Forgive me for not listening to her needs. Help me to trust you. Help me to trust my body. Amen.

Feed Yourself

"Is there anyone among you who, if your child asked for bread, would give a stone? Or if the child asked for a fish, would give a snake? If you, then, who are evil, know how to give good gifts to your children, how much more will your Father in heaven give good things to those who ask him!"

—Matthew 7:9-11

When I was in full diet-culture mode, my days would often fall into a particular pattern. I would spend the morning and early afternoon at work, eating like a rabbit and feeling pretty smug about whatever leafy food I had packed for myself. Then having starved myself all day, not surprisingly, around 3:00 p.m. I would crave something sweet. My body, quite in need of energy, was like Oliver Twist in a nineteenth-century workhouse saying, "Please, sir, may I have some more?" But instead of offering my body that energy, I would eat whatever abomination of a substitute I had packed for that day. A rice cake with a drizzle of fat-free chocolate syrup. A low-calorie yogurt. One of those 100-calorie packs of cookies that taste like sawdust. I would be completely unsatisfied and as grumpy as a viral internet cat.

I remember driving home from work one day during this time of my life. It was a Friday, and I watched people eating on restaurant patios, passing decadent appetizers, and sipping cocktails. They were smiling and laughing and free. And all I could do was pout. Why did they get to be free? Why did they get to eat delicious food and drink fabulous drinks?

When I look back on this now, I wonder why I would give myself a stone when I was hungry for bread. Why, when my body wanted a basket of fish and chips with a good wheat beer and a table of friends to share it with, would I give it a snake? And diet culture really does feel like a sneaky and deceptive snake. It becomes entwined with our desire to be virtuous and to feel as though we have control, and it twists itself around us until we are stuck in a tight coil of lies. The lies tell us that eating foods that satisfy us is a slippery slope. They convince us that if we do not keep a tight grip on our diets, then we will never stop eating. They tell us that because our bodies are shaped a certain way, we don't deserve to have freedom with food. But they are lies.

God wants to give us good gifts that include summer evenings on patios adorned with twinkling lights, eating heirloom tomatoes, fresh mozzarella, and crusty bread drizzled in olive oil. These gifts include bubbly drinks that come in special glasses and sharing a table with friends and loved ones. God's gifts include beauty and pleasure and satisfaction.

We can feed our bodies and our souls without succumbing to the lies of diet culture. There is no slippery slope. We deserve freedom and joy with food. God made our bodies with hunger cues and created our souls with a desire for connection and beauty. May we listen to those hungers and feed ourselves.

Nourishing God, help me to honor the hungers of my body and my soul. Forgive me for giving myself stones and snakes when I was hungry for bread and fish. Thank you for this wonderful body that knows how to tell me what it wants. Thank you for this soul that craves beautiful relationships. Help me to feed myself well. Amen.

Forgive Yourself

*Peter came and said to him, "Lord, if my brother or sis-
ter sins against me, how often should I forgive? As many as
seven times?" Jesus said to him, "Not seven times, but, I tell
you, seventy-seven times."*

—Matthew 18:21-22

Diet culture tells us that it's our own fault if we can't lose weight,
if we don't eat the "right" foods, if we don't exercise enough. It
says that if we could just stick to the plan, count all the points,
and do all the workouts, then we would have the body that
we've been told to want. But it's a rigged game. The diet industry makes
billions of dollars each year, knowing that at least 95 percent of intentional
weight-loss attempts fail. But they also know that we will blame ourselves
for our perceived failure instead of the diets themselves. We blame the
player instead of the game. Every time. And we don't just blame ourselves,
we get downright mean.

When I was fully indoctrinated by diet culture, I would often spend
mornings and afternoons restricting what I ate. By the time I got home
for dinner, I would be ravenous. So I would eat because I was too hungry
to try to restrict myself. And then I would berate myself for having no
willpower. I would go to bed filled with guilt, calling myself lazy and
things far uglier than that. But eating is not something we need to forgive
ourselves for. Nor is gaining weight or being hungry or skipping a workout

or taking a lengthy break from exercise for any reason at all or eating whatever and whenever we feel like it.

But there are things we need to release ourselves from. We can forgive ourselves for getting back on the diet bandwagon, for comparing ourselves to others, for restricting, for calling ourselves names, for using exercise as a punishment or compensation tool, for robbing ourselves of joyful experiences, for judging others' bodies or journeys, for not honoring our hunger, for using "health" as an excuse to harm ourselves, for not asking for help when we need it, for not receiving the compliment, for not receiving love. It can be difficult to acknowledge how hard we are on ourselves, let alone to offer ourselves forgiveness. But we don't hurt ourselves in isolation. These tendencies are a direct result of diet culture's influence. We are not wholly to blame; yet we still need to turn in a new direction. Grace abounds. There is more than enough mercy to cover this pain.

If you can't seem to manage offering forgiveness to yourself right this moment, hear this good news: In the name of Jesus Christ, you are forgiven! Glory to God. Amen.

> God of forgiveness, why is it so hard to forgive myself when I know you have already forgiven me? Help me to follow your words to Peter. Help me to forgive myself time and time again, as many times as I need to. Give me the wisdom to discern what needs to be forgiven and what needs to be released. Amen.

You Are Not
Too Much

A woman in the city, who was a sinner, having learned that [Jesus] was eating in the Pharisee's house, brought an alabaster jar of ointment. She stood behind him at his feet, weeping, and began to bathe his feet with her tears and to dry them with her hair, kissing his feet and anointing them with the ointment.

—Luke 7:37-38

Part of what drives us to dieting and trying to lose weight is a fear that we are too much. Our desires are too intense, our passions are too sensual, and our bodies are too big. We are taught to deny our desires and control our impulses. In diet culture, this translates to the belief that our bodies are shaped the way they are because we have no self-control. If we are in a higher weight body, then it must be because we eat too much or are lazy. At this stage in our Lenten journey together, we know that's not how it works. Being in a bigger body does not mean we are gluttonous. It does not mean we are lazy. It does not mean we are too much, even if the world around us thinks so.

Today's scripture passage from Luke offers us a glimpse of a woman that the world thought was too much. She was also viewed as impulsive, as lacking self-control, and as too sensual. This woman anoints Jesus' feet with oil and her tears and uses her hair to dry them. Jesus even says she was kissing his feet from the time she came through the door. What an over-the-top, sensual, bodily scene. There is touching and kissing and weeping and overwhelming scent. She is too much in so many ways—but not to Jesus. He describes her too muchness as a show of great love. He affirms her in her most too much moment.

Jesus affirms us too. Our bodies are not too much. Our hunger is not too much. Our desire is not too much. Our passion is not too much. We are not too much. Jesus does not want us to shrink ourselves. Jesus wants us to live fully with our whole bodies, with all their angles and curves and fleshiness and wrinkles and scars. All of it. We are not too much. We are just right.

God, sometimes I worry that I am too much. Help me to remember that you know all that I contain, and you love every little bit. When the world says I am too much, you say, "Leave her alone." Give me the courage to live fully into all you created me to be. Amen.

It's OK to Have a Bad Body Day

My brothers and sisters, whenever you face various trials, consider it all joy, because you know that the testing of your faith produces endurance. And let endurance complete its work, so that you may be complete and whole, lacking in nothing.

—James 1:2-4

f you have begun to explore the many wonderful body-positive social media accounts available (see the appendix for some examples), you may be left feeling like this journey is all sunshine and bikinis. Scrolling Instagram can have you believing that all these gorgeous women who have ditched diet culture now live in complete freedom and joy every day, eating and wearing and doing whatever they want. This is not the case. The path to radical self-love is a journey of ups and downs and in-betweens, and sometimes it downright stinks. This is hard work we are doing. Bad days will happen.

There will be days along this journey when our closets trigger a flood of tears. There will be times when we see ourselves in a candid snapshot, and it will cause us to doubt everything we have come to believe as true about our inherent goodness. There will be days when someone makes a comment that should make us angry but instead fills us with shame. There will be days when we are tempted to try a diet or a weight-loss scheme just one more time. There might be days when we actually do try a new diet or weight-loss scheme. There will be days when we are just sad that our bodies aren't what we want them to be or what the world tells us they should be.

But that is OK.

The bad days are moments to practice being gentle with ourselves. They are times to practice listening to what our bodies need and choosing to nurture them. The bad days offer us occasions to forgive ourselves, to make space for something that brings us joy, to go to bed early. These trials will build endurance in us. They will make us stronger so that the next time our closets or our inner monologues turn hostile, we won't be so easily knocked off-center. Working through the bad days will build a resilience that allows us to see beauty in that photo that once brought tears.

And the good news is bad days are only pit stops on this journey. They do not last. When we find ourselves amid a difficult body moment, we can remind ourselves that we will get to the other side. Like the psalmist says, "Weeping may linger for the night, but joy comes with the morning" (30:5).

God of refuge, the journey toward loving who you made me to be is not always easy. Some days I want to quit, but I know that quitting won't fix the hurt. Be my comfort when the road is hard. Dry my tears when I feel like they won't stop. Remind me that joy comes in the morning and that you walk with me through it all. Amen.

Body Freedom

For freedom Christ has set us free. Stand firm, therefore, and do not submit again to a yoke of slavery.

—Galatians 5:1

Christian freedom is less like "I get to do whatever I want! It's a free country!" and more like removing a strapless bra after a long day. It's that feeling of, "Ahhh, yes, this is who and what I'm supposed to be." Freedom from diet culture is similar. It *can* mean the freedom to eat an infinite number of cookies, if that's what your body is telling you it wants or needs. But even more so, it's the experience of realizing the door to the pantry was open the whole time and the only things between you and the cookies were lies. Once you know the door to the pantry is always open, you eat can cookies when you want and not feel ruled by them.

Living with a diet-culture mindset is living in bondage. It is believing a set of lies that keeps you restricted and rigidly stuck in obsessive thoughts and compulsive behaviors. God wants freedom for us. God wants us to have the mental space, the physical energy, and the time to live a life of joy, peace, and love. Diet culture steals these things and leaves us with a life of calorie counting, punishing exercise, anxiety, and never feeling good enough about ourselves. What a sad, limited existence, but we choose it because it feels like it's our only option. We don't know the pantry door is open.

Letting go of a diet-culture mindset can be scary because the world around us says that's how we gain acceptance. But that is a lie. Even though it's scary to let it go, freedom waits on the other side. Christian freedom tells us that we are loved and accepted just as we are. We don't have to lose one ounce or take one step on the treadmill to earn God's love. Letting go of these beliefs isn't easy, and it may be something we have to do again and again. Standing firm against the bondage of diet culture means a daily practice of centering ourselves in Christ's freedom and saying no to the yoke of restriction, scarcity, and suppression.

God of liberation, thank you for setting me free from anything that seeks to keep me trapped. Open my eyes so that I can see that freedom is available to me every day. Help me to stand firm when diet culture's lies try to woo me back into bondage. Amen.

Sunday

The First Supper

For most Christians, the phrase *The Last Supper* brings to mind Jesus' last meal before being arrested and crucified. We think of Jesus gathered in an upper room, sharing bread and wine with his closest followers and friends. It might also make us think of Leonardo da Vinci's famous renaissance painting or perhaps the Communion ritual that is central to Christian worship. But for many of us who have dieted off and on most of our lives, *The Last Supper* also references a familiar pre-restriction phenomenon—it is our last meal before we plan to go on a new diet. We know that restriction will begin the next day, so we eat all our favorite goodies in one last hurrah.

For today's spiritual practice, we will flip the script on the pre-diet "Last Supper." After all, Jesus' Last Supper was a bit of a misnomer in and of itself. What Jesus instituted at that table in Jerusalem was just the first of thousands of eucharistic feasts that take place each week in churches around the world. It is no mistake that a meal is one of the central symbols of our faith.

Food is one of the first ways we experience ourselves as loved and lovable. When we were infants and cried out in hunger, our parents fed us. During that feeding, we were held in warm arms, and we experienced love. Registered dietitian and social worker Ellyn Satter is a leading researcher of feeding and nutrition. She writes, "Eating and feeding reflect our attitudes and relationships with ourselves and others, as well as our histories.

125

Eating is about our regard for ourselves, our connection with our bodies, and our commitment to life itself." [2] I would add that feeding ourselves also reflects our relationship with God.

In Holy Communion, we trust that God will faithfully set the table and fill us to the brim with grace each and every time we show up. There is no restricting at the Lord's Table. There is no worrying if there will be enough or about when we will be able to feast again. One way we know we are loved is by how God consistently feeds us and nourishes us spiritually. God's grace is abundant. The Eucharist is a powerful and healing ritual that holds extra special significance for those of us who have struggled with food. Through Communion we are reminded that God always meets us at the table, and, in turn, we can know we will always be fed and we can feed ourselves.

I call this practice "The First Supper," though you can practice it as many times as you need and as often as you like. *First* is a relative term. It may be the first time *ever* you have freely fed yourself anything your body or heart desires. Or it may be the first time since the latest diet craze caught you with its sneaky, sticky fingers. In either case, this practice is always here to welcome you gently to the table. The practice takes the form of a meal and is accompanied by a table liturgy. [3]

Preparation

- Make a list of all the foods you love but have been keeping yourself from eating. Maybe you have told yourself they are "unhealthy" or "bad" for you. Maybe they are foods you fear, the ones you think you may never stop eating once you start. Write them down. If you are planning this with friends, you can make your lists together or separately, but make sure everyone participating has something on the list.

- Go out and get those foods! You can get a few favorites or go all in and procure the entire list. Just make sure to get enough that you can ensure you will be fully satisfied at the end of your meal.

Don't buy one dark chocolate raspberry truffle if you know you could eat a dozen. It's also best to do your shopping on the day of the supper. Your body changes from day to day, and what you crave in this moment may not be the thing you want two days from now. I understand that this part of the exercise may be cost restrictive. If this is the case, choose items off your list that fit your budget but still feel decadent. A single cupcake can be just as indulgent as an entire cheesecake.

- Set the table. This part is important. Don't just toss your goodies onto a paper plate or plan to eat them out of the package. Take time to be intentional about creating a sacred space for your meal. Make it beautiful. Use the good dishes. Maybe set out some fresh flowers or special artifacts that hold meaning for you. Set out at least one candle.

The Practice

- Light the candle(s), and pray the following blessing:
  - *God of abundance, bless this table. Let this be a meal of liberation and celebration. May it mark a new beginning. May it be the first of many joyful, Spirit-filled meals. May I/we eat with freedom and gratitude. Amen.*
- Read John 6:1-14 aloud.
  Jesus went to the other side of the Sea of Galilee, also called the Sea of Tiberias. A large crowd kept following him because they saw the signs that he was doing for the sick. Jesus went up the mountain and sat down there with his disciples. Now the Passover, the festival of the Jews, was near. When he looked up and saw a large crowd coming toward him, Jesus said to Philip, "Where are we to buy bread for these people to eat?" He said this to test him, for he himself knew what he was going to do. Philip answered him, "Two hundred denarii would not buy enough bread for each of them to get a little." One of his disciples, Andrew, Simon Peter's brother, said to him, "There is a

boy here who has five barley loaves and two fish. But what are they among so many people?" Jesus said, "Make the people sit down." Now there was a great deal of grass in the place, so they sat down, about five thousand in all. Then Jesus took the loaves, and when he had given thanks he distributed them to those who were seated; so also the fish, as much as they wanted. When they were satisfied, he told his disciples, "Gather up the fragments left over, so that nothing may be lost." So they gathered them up, and from the fragments of the five barley loaves, left by those who had eaten, they filled twelve baskets. When the people saw the sign that he had done, they began to say, "This is indeed the prophet who is to come into the world."

- Take time to consider your thoughts and emotional responses to the scripture reading. Here are a few prompts:
  - How did Jesus respond to the disciples' scarcity mindset? How have you operated from a place of scarcity when it comes to food?
  - The passage tells us that Jesus gave the people "as much as they wanted" and that they ate until they were satisfied. What does it mean for you to eat until you are satisfied?
  - When the people were satisfied, the disciples gathered up all the leftovers and filled twelve baskets. How can you learn to trust that you can feed yourself more food whenever you become hungry again?
- If you are dining in a group, go around the table and share what foods you brought and what it means for you to be eating them freely. If you are on your own, spend a moment thinking about why you chose these foods and what it feels like to eat them. Maybe jot down a few feelings or thoughts on paper.
- Close your mealtime with this prayer and extinguish the candle(s): *God of the table, thank you for all these good foods and for the ability to feed myself well. Thank you for the feeling of satisfaction and fullness. May I leave this table promising to return again anytime I need to be fed. Amen.*

This spiritual practice *can* be done alone, but I highly suggest you find a friend to join you. Better yet, a whole table of friends. I make this suggestion because diet culture tells us that eating our favorite foods is shameful. And shame thrives in isolation. For many of us, eating decadent and delicious food has been a secretive behavior, one that we would never dare allow others to see, at least not freely. We may take a tiny spoonful of our partner's dessert, mentioning that it's far too rich to eat the whole thing, while secretly craving a whole portion. Or we might agree to split a juicy burger with a friend even if we are ravenous. There is nothing shameful about feeding ourselves delicious food. Feeding ourselves is an act of deep self-love, but the lies of diet culture make us feel like we have to hide our true desires.

Ironically, being with others we trust and openly sharing the things we feel ashamed of is exactly the antidote to this shame spiral. Shame researcher Brené Brown says that shame and empathic presence cannot exist in the same space. She writes, "If you put shame in a petri dish and cover it with judgment, silence, and secrecy, you've created the perfect environment for shame to grow until it makes its way into every corner and crevice of your life. If, on the other hand, you put shame in a petri dish and douse it with empathy, shame loses its power and begins to wither."[4] So get your girlfriends together (the safe ones—not the judgy, fat phobic ones), and have a glorious feast. Sit around the table and talk about how good the food tastes. Trade stories about all the ways diet culture has robbed you, and make a pact to eat joyfully and freely together from this first supper onward.

Holy
Week

Holy Week

Eat Like a Kid Again

The disciples came to Jesus and asked, "Who is the greatest in the kingdom of heaven?" He called a child, whom he put among them, and said, "Truly I tell you, unless you change and become like children, you will never enter the kingdom of heaven."

—Matthew 18:1-3

When I was growing up, my dad worked for Nabisco, selling cookies to grocery stores. Sometimes I would go with him to the office where there was a whole closet of cookies of every flavor, shape, and texture, all for the taking. There was a lovely older lady with cropped salt-and-pepper curls who was tickled with delight to show me into that room and let me have my pick. I always picked Pinwheels—chocolate-covered marshmallow cookies with a graham cracker base. I'd open them as soon as I got home and gobble one up. It was pure deliciousness. The thing is, I don't ever remember sitting down as a six-year-old and eating a whole package. I might have had two, but I don't remember struggling with the fear that I would eat every single cookie.

But that was before I had any inkling of scarcity. It was before anyone told me I shouldn't have too many cookies "or else." It was before I was worried that I would gain weight or that cookies were "sinful" or that eating anything would make me "bad." I knew that when these cookies were gone, there was a nice lady with a closet full of cookies who would offer me more. Often the threat of restriction gives us the impulse to binge or feast.

Children—before the grown-ups mess things up—are intuitive eaters. They eat when they are hungry or when they are celebrating or when there is a party or when there is something that looks delicious. And sometimes a lollipop makes a skinned knee feel better. They stop when they are full or when they have had enough. If they are presented with full access to a range of foods, they eat what they need without bingeing or restricting. Checking the macros on a particular food would never occur to a child. Never would you hear a child say, "I've got to hit the playground and get in some reps on the monkey bars after eating all this mac and cheese."

At some point all those implicit and explicit messages about body size and how much food is OK and what foods are good or bad creep in and take hold of our brains. For many of us, we can't remember a time when those messages were not ingrained. Some of us may have been lucky not to hear the messaging at home, but we all have been exposed to it out in the world. For most women, the freedom of childhood eating and joyful movement comes to an end.

Jesus told his disciples that to enter the kingdom of heaven we must become like children. God recognizes the wisdom and purity of a child-like state of mind that hasn't been tainted by ego and our desire to fit in with the dominant culture. Children haven't yet been told that they cannot trust their bodies or that they are not good enough just as they are. To become childlike is to say no to unrealistic and narrow beauty standards and to say yes to honoring our bodies' cues and needs. Becoming like a child is to play and eat and move about creation with freedom and joy. So, go ahead—eat like a kid again.

God of joy, forgive me for forgetting what it
was like to eat and move like a child. Help me to
shed my belief in scarcity and the messages
of inadequacy from the world around me.
I want to eat freely and move joyfully again.
Help me to become like a child. Amen.

Spiritual Hunger

"Blessed are those who hunger and thirst for righteousness, for they will be filled."

—Matthew 5:6

t's my day off, and I'm wandering from room to room trying to fill whatever this nagging hole is. The house is quiet and still with the children at school and my husband at work. Afternoon sunlight is pointing out all the nooks and crannies that need to be dusted. I eat a snack. Nope, that didn't do it. I fiddle with my art supplies. Nope, not that either. I pick up a book and set it down. I scroll through my phone even though Instagram has already told me I'm "all caught up." I try another snack, salty and crunchy this time. Still no satisfaction. There is a hunger lingering in my body, hovering somewhere between my chest and my throat. I feel unsettled, antsy, and unsure how to scratch the itch.

It's not the first time I've felt this way. In fact, this low-grade rumbling often shows up when I find myself alone and at home in the afternoon. It's a confusing and restless feeling. It wants to be soothed, but nothing seems to soothe it. I know by now that this emptiness isn't a physical hunger, though that doesn't keep me from trying to feed it. It might be emotional or social hunger since it does bubble up most when I'm alone. But mostly I think it is spiritual hunger.

This spiritual hunger is a longing to be grounded in the Divine Presence. It is a desire to be held tightly but to be free at the same time. It is a wish to have every part of every cell feel deeply loved. It is a vibrating call to create but also to rest. And if I can be reflective in the moment and recognize what I am feeling is spiritual hunger, I can respond with spiritual practices. I can light a candle and pray or read scripture or meditate or do some yoga or take a mindful walk. But often I just curl up in a ball with my snacks and whatever British period drama I can find on PBS.

Separating spiritual hunger from physical hunger can be challenging. Sometimes it feels easier to feed myself pizza rolls that it does to feed myself through silent prayer. I will find myself in a pattern of responding to spiritual, emotional, or even intellectual hunger with food. When I do this, I end up feeling spiritually unfulfilled and physically uncomfortable. Becoming curious about what our bodies and souls need is a spiritual practice in itself. When we learn to identify what we are hungry for, we can feed ourselves well. Only when we honor all our hungers are we able to adequately nourish ourselves.

Nourishing God, thank you for all the ways you feed me. Forgive me for the times I ignore my spiritual hunger. Help me to discern my own hungers. Help me to know when I need a snack and when I need prayer time. Give me the strength and the will to choose what I need in each moment. Amen.

Body Privilege

There is no longer Jew or Greek; there is no longer slave or free; there is no longer male and female, for all of you are one in Christ Jesus.

—Galatians 3:28

Because of the many years I spent buying into diet culture, my own weight has fluctuated quite a bit during my life. Although I am the heaviest I have ever been and by no means identify as thin, I still have a great deal of thin privilege. By this I mean that I can shop in straight-sized clothing stores, I have no difficulty sitting on airplane seats or in restaurant booths, I have never had a doctor suggest weight loss to me, and rarely has someone made fun of me for my weight. It does not mean I haven't suffered deeply with body image and body shame. I definitely have, and there probably are not too many women around in this country who haven't had some type of struggle with loving their bodies. But my suffering is not equal to the suffering of those in higher weight bodies. I have the privilege of being able to go about my life with access to all the things I need and desire and without the threat of overt discrimination.

My thin privilege is also connected to my white privilege. The roots of fat phobia, especially in the United States, are found deep within the history of racism. The work of sociologist Sabrina Strings shows how during slavery, as White people sought to position themselves over and above Black people, the curvaceous figures of Black women became associated with fatness, and thus fatness became demonized.[1] Discrimination against fat bodies cannot be separated from the history of discrimination against Black bodies. Discrimination is a tangled, intersectional web that layers on more suffering for some than for others. To authentically address one form of oppression, we must address all of them.

Following Christ means that all the barriers are stripped away. We don't divide ourselves based on how we identify ourselves or how we look. Instead, all our beautiful, diverse bodies come together as one body in Christ. But to do that, those of us with privilege first need to become aware of it, to own it, and then use it to help bring about equity and to combat discrimination. It isn't enough to just *say* that in Christ there is no fat or thin, no White or Black, no rich or poor, no straight or queer. In fact, if we stop at these words, we run the risk of flattening this scripture into an erasure of our beautiful diversity. If we don't put these words into action, building a world where fat and thin bodies are treated equally, then these words can become a way of pretending our bodies are all the same while ignoring our differences and the injustices that many of us experience because of our bodies or identities. We have to work to create a world that isn't unaware of difference but is safe for and affirming of all people. That starts with rooting out the fear and prejudice that lives inside us, but it can't stop there. If you are a person with privilege, use it to make the world a more equitable place.

God of equity, you love each of us equally,
but we have created a world where some of
us suffer more than others. We are caught in
a web of assumptions, fears, and injustices.
Shed light on the parts of me where prejudice
lingers. Show me ways that I can work to
create peace and reconciliation. Change
me and change your world. Amen.

Maundy Thursday

God Loves You, Feet and All

[Jesus] poured water into a basin and began to wash the disciples' feet and to wipe them with the towel that was tied around him. He came to Simon Peter, who said to him, "Lord, are you going to wash my feet?" Jesus answered, "You do not know now what I am doing, but later you will understand." Peter said to him, "You will never wash my feet." Jesus answered, "Unless I wash you, you have no share with me." Simon Peter said to him, "Lord, not my feet only but also my hands and my head!" Jesus said to him, "One who has bathed does not need to wash, except for the feet, but is entirely clean. And you are clean, though not all of you." For he knew who was to betray him; for this reason he said, "Not all of you are clean." After he had washed their feet, had put on his robe, and had reclined again, he said to them, "Do you know what I have done to you? You call me Teacher and Lord, and you are right, for that is what I am. So if I, your Lord and Teacher, have washed your feet, you also ought to wash one another's feet. For I have set you an example, that you also should do as I have done to you.

—John 13:5-15

hate feet. I don't want anyone else's feet in my vicinity. I don't like the locker room at the pool where I know my feet will touch the same wet tiles that many other feet have touched. I know it's not body positive, but I just can't help it. My foot aversion is not usually a problem for my Christianity. That is—until Maundy Thursday.

Maundy Thursday is the day in the liturgical calendar where we remember how Jesus washed the disciples' feet. Many churches have foot-washing services on Maundy Thursday. Folks line up behind basins and take turns ceremoniously washing one another's feet. It's my own personal nightmare. I successfully have avoided this situation by "accidentally" wearing tights to any Maundy Thursday service I attend. This plan worked well when I lived in the Midwest. In Georgia, I take the chance of wearing tights on an 80-degree day. But I will take that gamble every time. Of all the sacramental acts Jesus could have picked, why did he have to wash feet? I suppose I've already answered this question. Jesus isn't afraid of feet because Jesus isn't afraid of or grossed out by any part of our bodies. And that means God, through Jesus, isn't either.

When my daughter was an infant, I caught a little glimpse of how God sees my body. When she was a baby, I would play all kinds of peeka-boo games with her. A favorite involved holding her pudgy pink toes in front of my face before I spread them apart and cooed at her. I would press her soft feet into my face and kiss their wrinkly soles, and she would giggle and giggle. One day I was about to shove that sweet little foot into my face, and I realized, *Wow—this is a foot. I don't hate ALL feet.* I love my baby girl's feet. As she grew older and those little feet would come home dirty and sweaty and stinky, I no longer wanted to put them on my face, but I surely didn't hate them.

Sometime between infancy and adulthood, we lose our ability to see our bodies as beautiful. Somehow our sweet little toes turn into adult-sized bunions. Like the proverbial frog in the pot, we soak in diet-culture soup until one day we realize we've been boiled into body loathing. All the implicit and explicit messages around us finally convince us that our bodies are not good enough. We start to notice all the parts of our bodies that we don't like or that we wish we could change. We start doing everything we can to change our bodies and make them conform.

But God still sees us with the same affectionate love that I felt when I pressed my little girl's soles against my cheeks. God sees those parts of our bodies and says, "I love that part of her!" Jesus loved his disciples in this way. He didn't hesitate to sit at their feet and gently wipe away the day's dirt and grime. Jesus poured cool water over them and patted them softly with clean towels. There was no part of his friends that Jesus was repelled by.

When you feel yourself criticizing some part of your body, remember how Jesus washed his disciples' feet. Imagine pouring love over that part of your body, just like Jesus poured water over those dirty toes so long ago. Remember that God loves every inch of you, even if you have trouble offering that same love to yourself.

God, my perfect Parent, teach me to see myself the way you see me. Help me to remember that you love each and every part of me. Soften my gaze when I look in the mirror. Help me to love the parts of me I dislike the most. Amen.

Good Friday

Body Love in the Shadows

It was now about noon, and darkness came over the whole land until three in the afternoon, while the sun's light failed, and the curtain of the temple was torn in two. Then Jesus, crying out with a loud voice, said, "Father, into your hands I commend my spirit." Having said this, he breathed his last.

—Luke 23:44-46

One late summer weekend I escaped the hot, sticky Atlanta heat and drove some winding switchback roads through the Appalachians of North Carolina to a United Methodist retreat center on the side of mountain. Four of my clergy friends joined me for a few days of writing. One morning while the hazy mist was still lingering amid the treetops, a friend and I sat in white rocking chairs, gazing out at the blue-green vista in front of us, and contemplated our mortality. I don't know how the conversation started, but before we knew it, we were sharing our fears and curiosities and close encounters with the end of life. Just as I said, "Well, we are all going to die at some point," a giant crow swooped down and landed in the tree right in front us. We both looked at each other like the Grim Reaper himself had just hooked us with his scythe. And if that were not enough, four of his friends followed him and began pecking at the ground in front of us. Remember, there were five of us staying in the house. Five crows, five clergy friends who are all going to die one day. Someone upstairs has a sense of humor.

Good Friday reminds us that death is part of the life cycle. Yes, this can mean literal death, but it can also mean metaphorical death—times when darkness is all around, and we feel afraid, worn down, and willing to believe the lies of diet culture. Learning to love our bodies will include a series of valleys and mountaintops, deaths and resurrections. We will need to forgive ourselves for being unkind to our bodies or not trusting them. We may find ourselves wounded and weeping when diet culture lands its blows, but we can celebrate when we choose to tell ourselves what is true: We are God's children, and our bodies are called very good.

Body love is a practice—a spiritual practice. And those times when we find ourselves in darkness or despair are important parts of the process. The shadows are the places where God meets us and transforms us. If we never move into the darkness, we do not have any appreciation for the light. Anyone who has struggled to internalize pithy platitudes about body love knows that we can't skip over the deeply wounded, angry, maybe even hateful places that linger inside of us. We can't strong-arm those parts away to get to a place of body love.

Like it or not, death is part of the deal. Yes, Easter is coming, but for now make some tender space for the parts of you that live in the shadows. Let the unkind, distrusting, self-loathing parts of you show their face and be known. Spend time writing about the darkness. Talk about it with someone you trust. Put on angry music and yell and dance and cry. Do whatever helps you enter the dark rather than avoiding it. Know that God enters that deathly place with you, holding you in the deepest love and grace. And the next time you see a crow, notice how even its blackest feathers shimmer with iridescent rainbows when they meet the light.

God, I don't want to face the dark parts of me. I don't want to acknowledge the angry, hurting, and ugly places I hold inside. Help me to brave the darkness of death, knowing that you are with me. Help me to trust that you love all of me— even my shadows. Show me your good news that resurrection is on the other side. Amen.

Holy Saturday

Body Justice

Let justice roll down like water
and righteousness like an ever-flowing stream.

—Amos 5:24

D iscrimination against those of us living in fat bodies remains a socially acceptable form of prejudice. The checkout lanes at the grocery store are filled with tabloid pictures of celebrities who dared to gain weight and show themselves in public. People with larger bodies regularly experience ridicule and name-calling just for walking down the street. Even well-meaning people say hurtful things to those of us with bigger bodies in the name of "concern for health."

Weight stigma has been shown to result in negative physical and mental health outcomes. People experiencing weight stigma are at risk of psychological disorders, pathological stress levels, and substandard health-care.[2] People in larger bodies face consistent discrimination and misdiagnosis in healthcare settings, which in turn creates hesitancy about engaging in the healthcare system at all. Being told you need to lose weight every time you had strep throat or a sprained wrist makes going to the doctor less than desirable. People in larger bodies are also less likely to be hired, and they make less money than their lower weight counterparts for doing the same work.[3] People in larger bodies face the lack of accessibility on airplanes and in restaurants, amusement parks, and theaters, which often results in humiliating exchanges or higher costs for purchasing extra seats or accommodations. Access to clothing that is attractive and comfortable and affordable is also a challenge for plus-sized people.

This world is unjust for people in larger bodies. But God calls us to be active participants in working for the justice of all people. If you are reading this book, you have likely suffered and struggled with your relationship with your body. Diet culture hurts us all. But that does not necessarily mean we all have experienced the full struggle of what it means to be fat in our society. Straight-sized and mid-sized people carry privilege that can be used to advocate and work for a world where justice does roll down like water.

If you are reading this book, you may also be one of God's children with a higher body weight who has experienced all of the above firsthand. God loves you and delights in your very existence. I repent for the ways I have been complicit in perpetuating weight-based injustice, and I hope everyone reading this will work for the day when we can all dip our toes in that ever-flowing stream of righteousness together.

God of justice, forgive me for participating in a culture that oppresses others and heal the hurts I have suffered from weight stigma. Show me how I can work to create a world that is just for and inclusive of all your children. Give me courage and resiliency to do that work. Amen.

Easter Sunday

Freedom Has Always Been Here

While they were talking and discussing, Jesus himself came
near and went with them, but their eyes were kept from rec-
ognizing him. . . . When he was at the table with them, he
took bread, blessed and broke it, and gave it to them. Then
their eyes were opened, and they recognized him.

—Luke 24:15-16, 30-31

ast year on my birthday a small group of friends gathered at a pop-
ular rooftop in downtown Atlanta. My birthday is in August, so it
was steamy. I knew I wanted to wear a pair of high-waisted jeans
paired with a tank top because of the heat. But even after years
of work dismantling diet culture in my own life and learning to love my
body as it is, I must have paced my bedroom floor hundreds of times that
afternoon, wondering if I could wear a form-fitting tank top. I tried putting a wrap over the top or replacing my jeans with a skirt that would hide
my belly. But I kept coming back to the outfit I actually wanted to wear.
Eventually I decided to go with my original plan—even as I felt a twinge
of fear and apprehension—and went out to celebrate. I wore the jeans and
tank top, and nothing bad happened. I stood on the rooftop and looked at
the Atlanta skyline while the breeze caressed my cardigan-free shoulders,

and the world did not collapse. I even received compliments on my outfit. Most of all, I enjoyed that night of sipping drinks and laughing with friends without letting diet culture consume my thoughts and behavior.

I tell this story knowing I have a great deal of body-size privilege. I know that for those of us in larger bodies, wearing what we want and are comfortable in can result in cruel comments from hateful bystanders. But I also know that those judgments do not have the last word on our worth. We can live a life ruled by the shame and fear and cruelty diet culture imposes on us, or we can choose to notice the freedom that is available to us and has been there all along.

Today's scripture passage comes from one of Jesus' resurrection appearances called the walk to Emmaus. The disciples have just discovered that the tomb is empty, and two of them are walking to the village of Emmaus. Jesus shows up and talks to them while they fret about all that has happened. The disciples do not recognize Jesus because we are told "their eyes were kept from recognizing him" (Luke 24:16). They are so caught up in their grief, fear, and confusion that they do not know that the One they long for is right beside them. Once they get to Emmaus, Jesus joins them for a meal. Yes, once again Jesus sits down for a meal with his followers. Jesus blesses the bread and breaks it, and only then do the disciples realize who has been traveling with them all that time.

Diet culture keeps us from noticing Christ in our midst—the real source of freedom and life who is always available to us. As I paced my bedroom that August afternoon, I was so focused on what my body looked like and how others might perceive it that I couldn't see the freedom that Christ offers to me. Letting go of diet culture's hateful messages allows us to see the goodness God has for us. God wants so much more for us than a diet. There is healing, wholeness, inspiration, creativity, relationship, love, joy, and peace on the other side. So let's sit down at the table, say a blessing, and break that bread. Thinness won't set us free, but Christ can.

God of resurrection, open my eyes to your freedom. Help me to trust that I can step out of the fear, shame, and judgment that diet culture imposes and to know that you will meet me there at the table. Thank you for walking with me, even when I couldn't recognize you. Amen.

Appendix

RESOURCE LIST

Books

Bacon, Linda, and Lucy Aphramor. *Body Respect: What Conventional Health Books Get Wrong, Leave Out, and Just Plain Fail to Understand about Weight.* Dallas, TX: BenBella Books, 2014.

Bennett, Ashlee. *The Art of Body Acceptance: Strengthen Your Relationship with Yourself Through Therapeutic Creative Exercises.* Salem, MA: Page Street Publishing, 2021.

Harrison, Christy. *Anti-Diet: Reclaim Your Time, Money, Well-Being, and Happiness Through Intuitive Eating.* New York: Little, Brown Spark, 2019.

Schauster, Heidi. *Nourish: How to Heal Your Relationships with Food, Body, and Self.* Somerville, MA: Hummingbird Press, 2018.

Scritchfield, Rebecca. *Body Kindness: Transform Your Health from the Inside Out—and Never Say Diet Again.* New York: Workman Publishing, 2016.

Strings, Sabrina. *Fearing the Black Body: The Racial Origins of Fat Phobia.* New York: NYU Press, 2019.

Taylor, Sonya Renee. *The Body Is Not an Apology: The Power of Radical Self-Love.* 2nd ed. Oakland, CA: Berrett-Koehler Publishers, 2021.

Tovar, Virgie. *The Self-Love Revolution: Radical Body Positivity for Girls of Color.* Oakland, CA: Instant Help Books, 2020.

Tovar, Virgie, and Lucile Perini. *The Body Positive Journal.* San Francisco: Chronicle Books, 2022.

Tribole, Evelyn, and Elyse Resch. *Intuitive Eating: A Revolutionary Anti-Diet Approach.* 4th ed. New York: St. Martin's Essentials, 2020.

Social Media Accounts

Anne Cumings (that's me!): @rev.annecumings on Instagram
Taco Belles (my body-positive Facebook Group):
    https://www.facebook.com/groups/thetacobelles
Christy Harrison: @chr1styharrison on Instagram and Twitter
Virgie Tovar: @virgietovar on Instagram and Twitter
Megan Jayne Crabb: @meganjaynecrabb on Instagram
Jes Baker: @themilitantbaker on Instagram and Twitter
Ragen Chastain: @ragenchastain on Instagram

Podcasts

Body Kindness
The Bodylove Project with Jessi Haggerty
Food Heaven
Food Psych Podcast with Christy Harrison

NOTES

Introduction

1. Sonya Renee Taylor, *The Body Is Not an Apology: The Power of Radical Self-Love*, 2nd. ed. (Oakland, CA: Berrett-Koehler Publishers, 2018), 6.
2. Roots of the body-positive movement existed in the mid-nineteenth century Victorian Dress Reform when women began to rebel against wearing corsets and other uncomfortable, structured garments meant to change the shape of the body to conform with cultural ideals. But it was in the 1960s when it began to take off as an organized movement.
3. R. Marie Griffith, *Born Again Bodies: Flesh and Spirit in American Christianity* (Berkeley, CA: University of California Press, 2004), 2.
4. Barbara Brown Taylor, *An Altar in the World: A Geography of Faith* (New York: Harper One, 2009), xv.
5. MissionInsite by ACS Technologies, *The MinistryInsite Priorities Report 2017*, prepared for North Georgia UMC, Tucker, GA, September 27, 2021.
6. Christy Harrison, *Anti-Diet: Reclaim Your Time, Money, Wellbeing, and Happiness Through Intuitive Eating* (New York: Little, Brown Spark, 2019), 7.
7. Sabrina Strings, *Fearing the Black Body: The Racial Origins of Fat Phobia* (New York: NYU Press, 2019), 6.

Week One

1. Christy Harrison, *Anti-Diet: Reclaim Your Time, Money, Wellbe-
    ing, and Happiness Through Intuitive Eating* (New York: Little,
    Brown Spark, 2019), 17.
2. Michelle M. Lelwica, *The Religion of Thinness: Satisfying the Spiri-
    tual Hungers behind Women's Obsession with Food and Weight*
    (Carlsbad, CA: Gürze Books, 2010).
3. See A. J. Stunkard and M. McLaren-Hume, "The Results of
    Treatment for Obesity: A Review of the Literature and Report of
    a Series," *AMA Archives of Internal Medicine* 103 (January 1959):
    85. https://jamanetwork.com; Suzanne W. Fletcher et al., "Meth-
    ods for Voluntary Weight Loss and Control," *Annals of Internal
    Medicine* 119, no. 7 (October 1993): 764.
4. Craig R. Koester, "Commentary on 1 John 4:1-6, *The Work-
    ing Preacher,* July 8, 2018, https://www.workingpreacher.org
    /commentaries/narrative-lectionary/preaching-series-on-1-john
    -3-of-4/commentary-on-1-john-41-6.
5. This may not feel accurate for those experiencing intrusive
    thoughts and/or mental illness. If that is you, I encourage you
    to find a mental health professional. A good place to start is the
    Find a Therapist function on the *Psychology Today* website. This
    search engine lets you sort by location, race, gender, therapeutic
    model, insurance coverage, and areas of expertise. https://www
    .psychologytoday.com/us/therapists.

Week Two

1. Anne Lamott, "A few quick thoughts on that diet you are about
    to fail," *The Washington Post,* January 1, 2018, https://www
    .washingtonpost.com/news/acts-of-faith/wp/2018/01/01/a-few
    -quick-thoughts-on-that-diet-you-are-about-to-fail/.

2. Xun Zhu, Rachel A. Smith, and Emily Buteau, "A Meta-Analysis of Weight Stigma and Health Behaviors," *American Psychological Association* 7, no. 1 (2022): 1.

3. Suzanne Simard, *Finding the Mother Tree: Discovering the Wisdom of the Forest* (New York: Alfred A. Knopf, 2021).

4. Paulina Swiatkowski, "Magazine influence on body dissatisfaction: Fashion vs. health?," *Cogent Social Sciences* 2, no. 1 (2016). https://www.tandfonline.com/doi/full/10.1080/23311886.2016.1250702?scroll=top&needAccess=true.

5. Michelle M. Lelwica, *The Religion of Thinness: Satisfying the Spiritual Hungers behind Women's Obsession with Food and Weight* (Carlsbad, CA: Gürze Books, 2010), 105.

Week Three

1. Evelyn Tribole and Elyse Resch, *Intuitive Eating: A Revolutionary Anti-Diet Approach*, 4th ed. (New York: St. Martin's Essentials, 2020), 229.

Week Four

1. Catherine McDowell, "In the Image of God He Created Them: How Genesis 1:26-27 Defines the Divine-Human Relationship and Why It Matters," in *The Image of God in an Image Driven Age: Explorations in Theological Anthropology*, ed. Beth Felker Jones and Jeffrey W. Barbeau (Downers Grove, IL: IVP Academic, 2016), 30.

2. Oswald Bayer, "Being in the Image of God," *Lutheran Quarterly* vol. 27 (2013): 79.

3. McDowell, "In the Image of God He Created Them," *The Image of God in an Image Driven Age*, 33.

4. Tertullian, "Modesty in Apparel Becoming to Women, in Memory of the Introduction of Sin into the World Through a Woman," from Book I in the Christian Classics Electronic Library, https://www.tertullian.org/anf/anf04/anf04-06.htm.

Week Five

1. Evelyn Tribole and Elyse Resch, *Intuitive Eating: A Revolutionary Anti-Diet Approach*, 4th ed. (New York: St. Martin's Essentials, 2020), 84.
2. Ellyn Satter, *Secrets of Feeding a Healthy Family: How to Eat, How to Raise Good Eaters, How to Cook*, 2nd ed. (Madison, WI: Kelcy Press, 2008), 1.
3. This liturgy is loosely based on The United Methodist Love Feast, which dates back to a German practice from the 1700s. https://www.umcdiscipleship.org/resources/the-love-feast.
4. Brené Brown, *Dare to Lead: Brave Work. Tough Conversations. Whole Hearts.* (New York: Random House, 2017), 160.

Holy Week

1. Sabrina Strings, *Fearing the Black Body: The Racial Origins of Fat Phobia* (New York: NYU Press, 2019), 6.
2. Rebecca M. Puhl and Chelsea A. Heuer, "Obesity Stigma: Important Considerations for Public Health," *American Journal of Public Health* 100, no. 6 (June 2010): 1019–28.
3. Euna Han, Edward C. Norton, and Sally C. Stearns, "Weight and Wages: Fat Versus Lean Paychecks," *Health Economics* 18, no. 5 (May 2009): 535–48.

CPSIA information can be obtained
at www.ICGtesting.com
Printed in the USA
BVHW031336011022
648424BV00006B/10